THE PROPHETIC TRUMP CARD

The God Factor in the U.S. Presidency

Randell Green

This book is © Copyright Randell Green 2019. All rights reserved. No part of this book may be reproduced without the express written permission of the author.

Scripture quotations taken from The Holy Bible, New International Version® NIV® Copyright © 1973 1978 1984 2011 by Biblica, Inc. ™
Used by permission. All rights reserved worldwide.

ISBN 978-0-6484879-0-6

Cover image by Comfreak
https://pixabay.com/photos/flash-lightning-weft-impact-weather-845848/

Many thanks to the assistance provided by Steve and Lynn with editing and formatting.

To Leonie – my best friend and wife, for your encouragement and support in all that I do.

Contents

Introduction	2
Chapter One: Prophets and Prophecy	6
Chapter Two: Policy and Politics	16
Chapter Three: Manifestations	31
Chapter Four: The 2007 Prophecy	47
Chapter Five: The 2014 Prophecy	65
Chapter Six: The Supreme Court Prophecy	80
Chapter Seven: The North Korea Prophecies	93
Chapter Eight: The Demise of Isis and Other Prophetic Words	99
Chapter Nine: Hope for Tomorrow	110
Recommended Reading	119

Introduction

It wasn't supposed to happen. An outsider, a flawed person, a man who some said was too rough around the edges and too crass when he spoke, won the race. Others claimed that he said things that were inappropriate, or not befitting of a person in his position. Sometimes his words were twisted by the news media, or taken out of context to mean more than what was said. Some described him as a Nazi and as a sexist, misogynist, racist, bigot. According to the media narrative, this man hates women, the disabled, Muslims, Mexicans and Latinos. Even worse, he would possibly cause a war and bring instability to America. Yet, with no experience in the world of politics, Donald J Trump pulled off the unthinkable and was elected President of the United States in November 2016, receiving more electoral votes than any other Republican candidate had received over the past thirty years. [1]

When he won, protestors hit the streets angrily proclaiming *"love trumps hate"* (I wonder if they saw the irony in that?) and "<bleep> Donald Trump." Others called for resistance and said he is *"not my President."* The frontpage headline for The Australian newspaper on Thursday 10th November 2016 said in big capital letters *"TRUMPED America stuns the world."* Further down the page another heading said *"Victory marks the revolt against the Establishment."* The Herald Sun headline about Trump's win was *"SHOCK AND AWE."*

Many were left wondering how could this happen?

On the day that Trump was sworn in as President the following January, protests erupted in Washington DC. During

---

[1] https://www.wnd.com/2017/01/actors-get-super-secret-training-on-how-to-bash-trump/#o2mzTIlg6i6kZyqL.99

a violent protest, a limousine was set on fire and destroyed by protestors. The limousine belonged to a Muslim man, one of the people groups the protestors claimed to be standing up for. A GoFundMe page was started to raise funds to help the Muslim limousine owner and many of the generous donors were Trump supporters.[2]

A group of white men walked into a restaurant in Washington DC around the same time, in town for Trump's inauguration. The waitress who served them was an African American lady who said she actually felt a bit prejudiced towards them when she found out the reason they had come to the city. One of the men in the group complimented her on her smile, and upon leaving they left her a $450 tip and a note. The note acknowledged their differences on *"certain issues"* and said if people could share a smile and kindness like the waitress displayed, then the country would *"come together as one people."* The waitress told the Washington Post, who reported this story, that she found these men, who were Trump supporters, more inclusive than her Left leaning friends. She believed they were also authentic when they spoke to her.[3] At the end of the day, who really demonstrated with their actions that love trumps hate?

Meanwhile, after Trump's stunning election victory, Christians both in Australia and America, were left wondering and divided on whether or not Trump's election win was a good thing.

Evangelist Franklin Graham posted on Facebook that secular media organisations were asking themselves, how did they miss it and how did it happen, that Trump won the election? He said they were stunned and some were in shock. *"None of them understand the God factor."* The God factor!

---

2   https://www1.cbn.com/cbnnews/us/2017/february/trump-supporters-lend-helping-hand-to-the-unlikeliest-of-people

3   https://townhall.com/tipsheet/guybenson/2017/01/25/awesome-trump-fans-leave-huge-tip-kind-note-for-stunned-antitrump-waitress-n2276893   and https://www.foxnews.com/food-drink/dc-waitress-overwhelmed-by-message-tip-left-by-trump-supporters

Did God really intervene in the U.S. elections? Graham added that whilst the media were trying to figure it all out, he believed that God had intervened in the American election. *"I believe that God's hand intervened Tuesday night to stop the godless, atheistic progressive agenda from taking control of our country."* [4] Former Alaska governor and 2008 VP candidate Sarah Palin said, *"No doubt, Divine Providence played a huge role in this election."* [5] Did God really play a role in the election of Donald Trump? If He did, then where's the proof? And if He did, why did He choose this man?

In the Old Testament book of 1 Samuel, the prophet Samuel is sent by God to anoint the future king of Israel. He arrives at the property of Jesse, believing that God has sent him to this family to anoint one of the sons to be the next king. He starts with the first son, thinking that this young man is the one. God tells him not to look at outward appearances, it's what's on the inside that counts. He goes through each of Jesse's sons but God rejects them all. Samuel asks if there is another son, and they bring in the youngest, a teenager who had been out minding the sheep. God says to Samuel, "This is the one, anoint him."

This story is a reminder that God at times picks the person no one else would pick because He sees more than what we do. And it also shows that there are times when God will send a prophet (or prophets) with a word about what He is about to do, and who or what He is going to work through.

---

4 Franklin Graham: They Didn't Understand The God Factor. 14 Nov 2016,

https://www.breakingchristiannews.com/articles/display_art_pf.html?ID=19729

and
https://www.facebook.com/FranklinGraham/posts/1304046609651517

5 Sarah Palin Says No doubt Divine Providence Played a Part In This Election. 28 Nov, 2016

https://www.breakingchristiannews.com/articles/display_art_pf.html?ID=19841 and https://www.breitbart.com/radio/2016/11/25/sarah-palin-grateful-see-church-step-donald-trump-eight-years-ago-felt-didnt/

That's what this short book is about – what God revealed to some prophets about the election of Donald J Trump as President of the United States.

Chapter One

Prophets & Prophecy

Before I take you through the prophecies spoken in the past regarding a future American President, it would be helpful for us to be on the same (prophetic) page. There are many voices in the world today predicting the future or interpreting what is going on around us. We have expert predictions on an array of topics including economics, the environment and politics. We have psychics and astrologers predicting the future, the prognosis of media commentators and then, we have in the church, prophets and those who move in the prophetic gifting.

I have listened to many teachings, and read a few books, about prophets and prophecy over many years, from various prophets and teachers. I have been inspired and informed by many speakers on this subject such as the late Kim Clement. I hope I do it justice when I pass onto you what I have learned.

Amos 3:7 says, *"Surely the sovereign Lord does nothing without revealing his plan to his servants the prophets."* Do you want to hear some good news? God is revealing things to His prophets who are active today in the church. Of all the people in the community, we the church should be the ones with the most hope because God's Word is the hope of the world. According to this verse in Amos, God will reveal what He intends to do through his prophets. Ephesians 2:20 says that the church is built on the foundation of the apostles and prophets while Ephesians 4:11-12 tells us that the office of the prophet is one of the ministry gifts God has given to equip believers to do the work of the ministry. In

1 Corinthians 14, the apostle Paul encourages us to be eager for the gifts of the Spirit, especially prophecy, although this is different to the office of a prophet, which is one of the five-fold ministry gifts. Paul was called by God to be an apostle and in the same way, some are called to be pastors, evangelists, teachers or prophets.

When it comes to prophecy, as in foretelling the future, the word of God is our benchmark. Only God knows the future, not psychics, mediums, astrologers, witches, not even Satan. For example, in Isaiah 46:10a God categorically states only He knows the future. *"I make known the end from the beginning, from ancient times, what is still to come."* Isaiah 48:6b says God will tell us of hidden and new things that we could not know about. Isaiah 42:9 God says, *"See, the former things have taken place, and the new things I declare; before they spring into being, I announce them to you."* And in Isaiah 44:7, God throws down a challenge. *"Who then is like me? Let him proclaim it. Let him declare and lay out before me what has happened since I established my ancient people, and what is yet to come – yes, let him foretell what will come."*

The first thing to establish then, is that only God knows the future. Secondly, God works through people and so the Holy Spirit prophesies through people. We see this throughout scripture. In Numbers 11:25, seventy elders prophesied when the Holy Spirit came on them. Old Testament prophets such as Jeremiah, Ezekiel and Isaiah all acknowledge that God gave them the words to speak.

We are not meant to reject prophecy but neither are we to accept every word a prophet speaks. 1 Thessalonians 5:20-21 says that we are not to scoff at or despise prophecy, but to test everything that is said and hold onto what is good. To hold onto what is good infers that someone prophesying may not always get it right. The human factor comes into play in prophecy. Sometimes we can prophesy out of our own beliefs, for example we prefer one political candidate over another, and so we prophesy the one we favour to win. Been there, done that.

The late Kim Clement prophesied in the mid 1990's that a burning bush would lead America. He said he was not impressed with George W. Bush as a governor at the time he gave the prophecy. However, when that word came to him, he recognised it must have been a word from God because Bush was not someone he would have picked.

If prophecy was plainly spoken, there would be no need to judge it. And if it was as clear as day, then there would be no need to seek God for the understanding. And let's face it, we are only human and we don't always get it right. If we get it wrong, does that then make us a false prophet, pastor, minister or Christian? In the Bible, there are examples of godly prophets who didn't quite get it right, yet they were never disqualified from their prophetic role. In 2 Samuel 7:2-5, King David summons the prophet Nathan and says that he is thinking of building a temple for the Ark of God, which at that stage was kept in a tent. Nathan tells David to go ahead and do whatever he has in mind, because God is with him. But, that same night, the Lord says to Nathan, "Go and tell David that he is not the one to build a temple for me, his son will." Nathan felt, believed, or had an impression that building a temple for God was the right thing to do, but his word to David wasn't spot on, and God had to give a clarifying word to him.

Consider Jonah. God sends him to the city of Nineveh with a prophetic word that the city will be destroyed because of its wickedness, yet the people repented and God delayed the destruction of the city. Does that make Jonah a false prophet? Of course not! However, after God had seen the repentant heart of the people, He changed the plans. In 2 Kings 20, the prophet Isaiah warns King Hezekiah to get his house in order because he was going to die from his illness. Hezekiah calls out to God, and God changes the plan and directs Isaiah to go back to Hezekiah and tell him, "I will give you another fifteen years." Again, another prophecy (get your house in order) does not come to pass.

We find the same again in Acts 21. A prophet by the name of Agabus takes the apostle Paul's belt and binds his own hands and feet with it. Then he says to Paul that he will be bound by the Jewish leaders and turned over to the Gentiles. However, the prophecy does not play out this way because Paul is grabbed by an angry mob who drag him from the Jewish temple and try to kill him. Only the timely arrival of Roman soldiers saved him, when they arrested him and took him to safety. In other words, Paul wasn't handed over by the Jews to the Romans, the Romans had to rescue Paul from being killed by the Jews.

Was Agabus then a false prophet? No. His word did come to pass in that an event did happen in Jerusalem that ended up with Paul being handed over to the Gentiles. How that event played out was slightly different to how Agabus saw it yet he did discern something in the Spirit and related it as best he could.

It is important to understand this because prophets can sometimes prophesy one thing but it may not transpire word for word. If you do a search on Google for 'false prophet', you may (or may not) be surprised as to who is considered a false prophet by sincere but sincerely wrong believers. I've seen it written about well-established and respected ministry leaders like evangelist Billy Graham, South Korea's Yongi Cho, prophet Cindy Jacobs, Morning Star Ministries founder Rick Joyner or Christian singers like Michael W Smith and Toby Mac. The list goes on.

So, what are the telltale signs of a false prophet? In a nutshell, a biblical prophet is someone who hears from God and relays that message to other people. How many of you reading this book believe you have heard from God during your time as a Christian? And how many can say you got it wrong a few times, even when you thought beyond a shadow of a doubt that you had heard from God? You thought God was telling you one thing but another happened or didn't happen. Did you misunderstand something? I know I have gotten a few things wrong over the years, just ask my wife and kids. Does that then make me a false Christian?

Getting a prophecy wrong or not having it come to pass does not automatically mean someone is a false prophet. Deuteronomy 13 gives us a guide on how we can assess a true prophet from a false. Firstly, we read in the first two verses that a false prophet can actually have a sign or wonder take place, something that looks like a miracle. But both true and false prophets can produce signs and wonders. We read in Exodus for example, that Moses and Aaron are performing signs and wonders right along with Pharaoh's magicians, although Pharaoh's magicians were limited in what they could do. In Deuteronomy 13 and verse 2, we get the clue as to how we are to define a false prophet. That is, they will say, *"Let us follow other gods and worship them."* This was what Pharaoh's magicians did. They worshipped other gods and therefore they qualified as false prophets, not because of the signs and wonders, but because of the worship of these other gods.

Does this passage then teach that a prophet whose prophecy did not come to pass warranted the death penalty for getting it wrong? Verse 5 says that a prophet or dreamer (who leads people astray to worship other gods) must be put to death because they have incited rebellion against God. It wasn't for getting the prophecy wrong that the prophet was to be executed. It was leading the people astray to worship other gods that warranted the death penalty. That law applied to both people claiming to be prophets and anyone else (in verses 6 to 11) who tried to lead the people astray to worship other gods. The death sentence was intended to prevent Israel from being enticed to follow other gods that would lead them into deviant and wicked practices that God did not want his people to follow.

In Deuteronomy 18, the people are asking Moses how

to recognise a false prophet. Moses lays out some ground rules. First of all, verse 18 says that God will put His words in the mouth of a prophet. In verse 20, we read that anyone who presumes to speak in God's name (such as a self-proclaimed prophet, not a God ordained prophet) or in the name of other gods, was to be put to death. However, verse 22 says that if something a prophet says does not come to pass, then don't be alarmed. If it was from God it would come to pass, if it wasn't from God it would not come to pass. Seasoned prophet Kim Clement, writes that there was no need to stone a prophet if their word did not come to pass since the word had no credibility. [6] One last point from Deuteronomy is in verse 19. In this verse, God says that if anyone does not listen to what the prophet has spoken in God's name, He will hold that person to account. A sobering thought.

Clement teaches that sometimes the Holy Spirit will give prophecies that at first appear contradictory. For example, Isaiah says that the Messiah will come from Galilee, Hosea says that he will be called out of Egypt, while Micah says that the Messiah will come from Bethlehem. All of these things were true at different times in Jesus' life. We need to allow prophecy to unfold and it has to be perceived spiritually. Sometimes God gives us a different outlook on situations.

In 1989 I received a personal prophetic word that in the days to come God would set me among the leaders in the house of God. Firstly, I had already been involved in church leadership since I was seventeen as a youth leader, but this prophecy was talking about something at the next level. The "days to come" took ten years, so it wasn't referring to literal days, but rather a passage of time. In 1999 I was asked to come onto the senior leadership team at the church I had been attending since I was nineteen. That was a fulfilment of the 1989 prophecy. But it didn't stop there. Approximately ten years later, I attended a regional meeting of CRC pastors

---

6 Call Me Crazy But I'm Hearing God, Kim Clement, Destiny Image Publishers, 2007, pgs 78, 79.

(CRC Churches International is the denomination I have been involved with since 1982) and, at that first meeting I recalled the 1989 prophecy. Here was another level to it. Around the same time, I became involved with the monthly meetings held by the minister's association in Traralgon where I live, so, once again I was sitting with the leaders in the house of the Lord. As already mentioned, prophecy has to unfold and it has to be spiritually perceived. My 1989 prophecy has had more than one application.

Clement describes prophecy this way: Imagine you are standing in a room at night with no lights on when, all of a sudden, there is a flash of lightning. In the moment of that flash you see a table, a TV and a shelf. It's not all clear, you may not get all the detail, but you have seen something or, you have heard something in the Spirit. Prophecy can be like this, a glimpse, sometimes with detail, sometimes not. Proverbs 25:2 says, *"It is the glory of God to conceal a matter, to search out a matter is the glory of kings."* God wants us to search things out, to dig deeper and enquire of Him. Numbers 12:6-8 says that God does not always make things plain. Sometimes He speaks in riddles or not clearly, sometimes in visions and dreams, although with Moses He spoke clearly and face to face. Jesus often spoke in parables to the people and then later explained the meaning of the parables to His disciples. Paul writes in Corinthians that we only know in part, so prophecy is not always like picking up a book and reading a sentence plainly. This is the way that God does it. That does not mean everything is a riddle or that everything is hard to understand. If everything we received in prophecy were easy to understand, or made sense, then there would be no need for faith and no need to judge the words as Paul instructs us to do in Thessalonians.

So why does God give us prophetic insight? Prophecy can give us a future and a hope, to show us things so that, when they happen, even if we do not understand or like what we are seeing, we can at least say, God has things in hand. It can help us make sense of a world that sometimes seems crazy. When we listen to media reports with their bias and single focus issues, and not what God has said through his prophets, it is easy to miss what God is doing.

Sometimes teaching on bible prophecy around the 'last days,' has led to people not planning for their future. Case in point, a fellow pastor and I stood as candidates for the minor political party Family First in the 2016 Federal election. He told me that a fellow believer told him that there was no point getting involved in politics because Jesus was coming back soon. What this person may not have realised is that many believers over the centuries have believed the same thing. They all believed Jesus was coming back in their day. I recall reading end times books in the 1980s, with the eager expectation that Jesus would return by the year 2000, reading the predictions of various authors as to when certain events, such as the rapture, were going to occur. Kim Clement said we have a choice – to see the gloom and doom or to *"see the light in the dark place."* We need to ensure we don't disengage from society. After all, Jesus gave us the Great Commission to go into the world, not withdraw from it.

So, why does God reveal things to us? To give us hope. Clement said that the enemy (i.e. Satan) does not want us to know that God has hope for us. God also reveals things to us so that we can pray and act. In Acts 11 the prophet Agabus prophesied that a famine was coming. The believers responded by providing help to those affected. Cindy Jacobs teaches that God sometimes warns us of things that are coming to help prepare, or so that we may pray to avert. Clement calls this prophetic preservation. When Daniel knew that the time for the seventy-year prophecy of captivity for Israel was nearing completion, he began seeking God in prayer for the next part of the prophecy to be fulfilled. We can take prophetic words and put them into action through prayer.

For example, God may give a prophetic warning about a terrorist attack so that His people will respond in prayer so that the attack is either averted, or the damage becomes minimal, or even just as a warning to prepare. There might be a call to pray for a nation or an event, or a word given in advance that this is God's plan for the future. The prophetic word and our response can make or break the fulfillment of it. Prophecy, especially personal prophecy, can also be ignored or it can be forfeited if we fail to act upon it. A prophetic warning not heeded may result in tragedy. A prophetic word about a family member coming to faith in Christ does not mean God will override that person's free will. However, it should spur us on to pray so that the person can come to faith, because God is willing that none should perish.

In 2017 I received a prophetic word at a meeting from a visiting speaker from Canada. Part of what he said was, *"You're about to have a new day."* That got my attention because, five years earlier, a visiting speaker at our church prophesied over my wife and I that we were at the dawn of a new day. But then the prophet from Canada said, *"The enemy tried to take you out, it wasn't God, you're fine."* I walked away wondering what is he talking about? When did the enemy try to take me out, past tense? Fast forward to 2018 and my doctor carried out some tests after I reported feeling strangely unwell. During the tests it was discovered that I had a large, cancerous tumour growing on one kidney. The scans were taken on the Wednesday, on the Friday the doctor gave me the results and then, on Sunday morning, I re-read the prophecy from 2017. I left for church that morning somewhat encouraged after re-reading the prophecy and, when I got to church, one of the men from our midweek prayer group pulled me aside. He told me that he and others at the prayer meeting on the Wednesday night (the day I had the scans done), not knowing about my health situation, had been praying for me and my family. He believed that the enemy had been attacking me to stop me from seeking the Lord, and the Lord was saying to press in and trust Him. This lined up with the prophecy I had received the year before, and I realised then that I had been given a prophetic glimpse of the future. This was prophetic preservation. With those prophetic words, I knew that my outcome was going to be good even though at first the prophecy did not seem clear. The operation to remove the tumour was a success although one kidney could not be saved. It did not take as long as expected (four and half hours instead of the six or seven estimated) and there are no indications that any microscopic elements of the cancer remain. I now have to have scans and tests done into the foreseeable future. However, I have hope and trust in God because of the prophetic word.

Summarising then what we have covered so far, there are a number of things to keep in mind when hearing, reading, discerning and praying about prophecy.

* God reveals what He is doing through His prophets.
* Only God knows the future.
* The Word of God is our benchmark.
* The Holy Spirit prophesies through people.
* Prophecy is not always plain and easy to understand.
* The Human Factor – prophets do not always get the prophetic word right or can be wrong altogether.
* The key point about a false prophet is that they are someone who leads people astray to worship other gods.
* Prophecies can sometimes appear contradictory.
* Prophecy has to unfold and has to be spiritually discerned.
* The prophetic anointing carries the future.
* Prophecy gives hope.

Having now covered some prophetic principles, let's delve into some of the prophetic words given regarding the 2016 Presidential elections in America. The key points we have covered in this chapter will help us in understanding the prophecies and assessing events that have unfolded since the prophecies were given.

Chapter Two

Policy & Politics

Stephen Mansfield in his book, *Choosing Donald Trump,* provides an overview of Donald Trump, the man. He writes about his upbringing, his personality, the nicknames his father gave him (*King & Killer*) and the people who have influenced, or currently influence him. He also presents a case that part of the reason Trump was elected in 2016, was due to anger among the Christian community about where their nation was headed. (Anger or intercessory burden?) Anger is not a bad thing in and of itself. The apostle Paul writes in Ephesians 4:26 that in our anger, do not sin.

    Mansfield writes about the pastor of a large church of several thousand in Las Vegas, made up of 30% Hispanics and 30% African Americans. This pastor was very concerned about candidate Trump in 2016, offended by his speech and actions. After one of the church's Hispanic team members met with Donald Trump and told him that he did not understand Hispanic people, Trump asked what could he do to get to know them better. This eventually led to Trump coming to visit the church school. Here he spent time listening to former gang members, a decorated and disabled war veteran and a children's choir, with students stepping forward to shake his hand. Those present commented afterwards that Donald Trump *"is nicer in person"* and *"so gentle and kind one on one."* This is similar to other comments I have read such as *"gracious, non-confrontational and open to give and take."*[7] You might be asking are we talking about the same man?

It was the media at the Las Vegas visit though, who didn't let the truth get in the way of a good story. One journalist asked the pastor what he thought of the protests at the school when there were none. Another newspaper reported that Trump had terrorised second graders, and another that the pastor had been paid by Trump for the visit. Only one media outlet reported the facts.[8] Much of what the media has reported has been slanted against Trump. Whatever we might think about Trump, reviews of the media's reporting in the U.S. showed that 80 to 90 per cent of the coverage is generally negative or critical. How can we cut through all the news reporting and get to the real issues? Who is influencing you and me? Jesus said in Mark 4:24 to be careful who we listen to. In this book my aim is to present a perspective from a prophetically spiritual standpoint. Perhaps we will be able to say, God has things in hand and He is in this situation. It's not the end of the world and there is hope for a better tomorrow, despite the turmoil we constantly hear through the nightly news broadcasts.

At the beginning of 2016, the Apostolic Council of Prophetic Elders (ACPE) from the United States released a lengthy word for that year as they have done for many years. This prophetic word dealt mainly with the United States however, part of it was for other nations, and there were parts of the word that could have applied generally. One of the themes in the word was that 2016 would be the year that the tide turns. Events were going to occur that would see a turning, a change of direction for God's kingdom here on earth. They referenced Isaiah 59:19b about how God would

---

7 https://www.charismanews.com/opinion/59304-donald-trump-key-to-isaiah-45-prophecy

8 Choosing Donald Trump, Stephen Mansfield, Baker Books, 2017, pgs 152-56

raise up a standard when the enemy comes in like a flood. They said the tide will turn against the enemy's plans, and a divine reversal will take place. It goes on to say that hidden agendas will be revealed in those who are inflaming riots and it will shock. *"The riots are not over in the United States. We must pray for the United States so there will not be mass riots that disrupt the elections."* [9]

During October 2016, conservative activist group, Project Veritas, released video clips of some of the undercover work they had completed over the previous twelve months. Veritas journalists had infiltrated two political consulting companies with ties to the Democratic party. The videos revealed that Democratic operatives had been infiltrating Trump political rallies to deliberately stir up trouble in order to make Trump supporters look bad. For example, operatives would attend Trump rallies wearing Nazi shirts or Planned Parenthood t-shirts to try and get a violent response from Republican supporters. The violence was planned in advance to take place in front of the TV cameras so Trump supporters would be reported as angry and violent people. Homeless and mentally ill people were paid to cause trouble, along with union members and people who believed in the cause.

The founder of the Foval Group, Scott Foval, one of the organisations involved in disrupting the rallies, said they needed to win the election regardless of what the legal and ethics advisers would say. Foval was later sacked. The videos revealed that there were links to the Democratic party and the people who were inciting the violence.[10] Cartoonist Scott Adams claimed that the unifying characteristic he had seen

---

9 https://www.generals.org/articles/single/word-of-the-lord-for-2016/

10 https://townhall.com/tipsheet/cortneyobrien/2016/10/18/second-veritas-video-dnc-operatives-admit-theyve-rigged-elections-for-half-a-century-n2234110 and https://www.projectveritasaction.com/video/rigging-the-election-video-iii-creamer-confirms-hillary-clinton-was-personally-involved/ and https://www.heraldsun.com.au/blogs/andrew-bolt/hillarys-dirty-tricks-exposed/news-story/c947499d9f6a45c1f053e101326b6bd4

from Clinton supporters was a willingness to bully. Trump signs were stolen, cars with Trump bumper stickers were defaced, people sacked from jobs if they spoke in favour of him, while the media downplayed all these forms of bullying and intimidation against Trump supporters.[11]

Interestingly, what we have seen since the 2016 election campaign has been protests, riots, harassment and anger displayed by those opposed to Trump. Some have explained this behaviour as coming from people who are angry and scared for their future, and who believe a big injustice has been committed. Therefore, the anger is justified. If one believes that Trump is evil, a Nazi or a bigot, then one could reason that non-civil actions are justifiable. There have been reportedly smaller numbers of Trump supporters heckling or swearing at Democratic politicians but, these are seemingly carried out by a few and have been condemned by Republicans.[12] I'm not saying that all Democratic supporters are violent or involved in bullying, harassment or intimidation, that would be a rash generalisation. And it would be unfair towards the law-abiding Democratic party supporters and politicians. The same would apply to Republican politicians and supporters. If we judge the whole group by the few we will end up in error.

The ACPE's word for 2016 also touched on abortion and about *"... advances toward the overturning of Roe vs. Wade,"* (the court case that helped to legalise abortion in 1973.) The ACPE believes that *"God has a case that, once presented in the courts, will make it extremely difficult to get an abortion in the nation."* The Hyde Amendment was passed in America in 1976 to allow Federal funding of abortions

---

11 https://www.heraldsun.com.au/blogs/andrew-bolt/clinton-leads-the-party-of-bullies/news-story/9adc3a1d7458748fa7655a27831062d9

12 https://townhall.com/tipsheet/cortneyobrien/2018/10/22/pelosi-gets-harassed-outside-campaign-event-n2530845 and https://www.independent.co.uk/news/world/americas/midterm-elections-2018-nancy-pelosi-far-right-hecklers-communist-disrupt-florida-campaign-a8593311.html

where the abortion was required due to incest, rape, or to protect the mother's life. This is approximately 0.5% of all abortions in America, meaning other reasons (including not ready and financial situation) are why abortions are performed. The Hyde Amendment with a forty-year life span was due to be reviewed in 2016. Democratic Presidential candidate Hillary Clinton promised to repeal the Hyde Amendment,[13] and this was also part of the Democratic party's election platform. The Democratic Party believed that the Hyde Amendment was an impediment to women obtaining abortion services. They wanted to remove all restrictions to abortion, including the free speech of pro-life street counsellors, and to continue funding for abortion providers including Planned Parenthood. The Democrats maintained this position, even after the exposure of Planned Parenthood's harvesting of aborted baby body parts for profit, which is illegal in the U.S. In some cases, babies born alive from failed abortions, are being killed and then harvested for body parts.[14] Early in 2019 the states of New York and Virginia legalised full term abortions, with the Virginia bill allowing abortion up to the point of birth, with some labelling this legalised infanticide.[15] Donald Trump on the other hand said he was going to appoint justices to the Supreme Court who will have great intellect and

---

13 Democratics Adopt Most Pro-Abortion Platform In History 28 Jul 2016, https://www.breakingchristiannews.com/articles/display_art.html?ID=18801 and https://www.generals.org/articles/single/word-of-the-lord-for-2016/

14 Planned Parenthood Horror Videos Investigation Underway As Congressional Hearing Begins 10 Sep 2015
https://www.breakingchristiannews.com/articles/display_art.html?ID=16652 and Breaking: Planned Parenthood Caught In New Video 'We Make Fair Amount Selling Fresh Baby Eyes, Gonads,' 15 Sep 2015, https://www.breakingchristiannews.com/articles/display_art.html?ID=16678   and https://www.washingtonpost.com/news/acts-offaith/wp/2015/07/15/ congressional-state-investigations-into-planned-parenthood-underway-after-undercover-video-goes-viral/?noredirect=on&utm_term=.04f08b0f20cd

15 Virginia Late Term Abortion Bill Labelled 'Infanticide.' 31 Jan 2019 https://www.bbc.com/news/world-us-canada-47066307

who will also be pro-life. [16] The Republican Party's position is, *the unborn child has a fundamental right to life which cannot be infringed.*[17]

This is significant as appointments to the U.S. Supreme Court are for life. The appointment of pro-life judges or pro-abortion judges by any President can affect the next generation. There are a few judges on the U.S. Supreme Court who, because of their age and or their health, may soon retire from the court. Of the nine judges who made up the court in 2016, four were conservative (with one actually passing away early that year, reducing their number to three), four were progressive or left leaning judges, and the remaining judge was a swinging voter. On the 22nd of January 2018, National Sanctity of Human Life Day, President Trump made a proclamation, as hundreds of thousands of pro-life supporters descended on Washington DC. He said, *"Reverence for every human life, one of the values for which our Founding Fathers fought, defines the character of our Nation."* The reason for National Sanctity of Human Life Day, said Trump, is *"to affirm the truth that all life is sacred, that every person has inherent dignity and worth, and that no class of people should ever be discarded as non-human."*[18]

Before the 2016 election, Hugh Hewitt, a professor of law and media commentator, noted that, under a Clinton presidency, every issue would end up in the Supreme Court for a court ordered solution to every social problem. This would result in governmental and judicial overreach into every area of life. Dr Lance Wallnau wrote that we live in a time of moral

---

16 At Meeting With Evangelicals Trump Promises We Are Going To Appoint Great Supreme Court Justices, And They Will Be Pro-Life https://www.breakingchristiannews.com/articles/display_art.html?ID=18504 22 June 2016, and Pence: Roe v Wade Will Be Overturned After Trump Elected. https://www.breakingchristiannews.com/articles/display_art.html?ID=18812 29 July 2016

17 Billy Graham Association Releases 2016 Voting Guide. https://www.breakingchristiannews.com/articles/display_art.html?ID=19023

18 https://www.lifesitenews.com/news/trump-declares-roe-v.-wade-abortion-anniversary-to-be-sanctity-of-human-life

relativism and culture wars, where the meanings of words such as marriage and gender are being changed. He predicted that even the term freedom of speech would become known as hate speech in the future. When it came to the Supreme Court, the 2016 election would give *"the victor the ultimate spoils."*[19] More about the Supreme Court in chapter six however, the issue of appointments to the court became a battlefield in 2018. Trump's nominated judge for the Supreme Court, Brett Kavanaugh, faced allegations of sexual assault. The Democratic party fought a delaying tactic tooth and nail with a smear campaign, not because the judge was unqualified for the Supreme Court, but because of a loss of power and influence if another 'conservative' judge was appointed. Another conservative judge, Neil Gorsuch, had been appointed in 2017. Kavanaugh's eventual appointment late in 2018, boosted the number of conservative justices on the court from four to five out of nine.

In relation to religious liberty, Trump said during his 2016 election campaign that he would protect people's right to say Merry Christmas, [20] and to defend religious freedom. In a pre-election TV commercial, he said Christians in America were under attack, they were persecuted and marginalised, while Christians overseas were being killed for their faith. The 2016 election was going to decide life, liberty and faith in America, rights that Trump said he would defend.

Trump also spoke about repealing the Johnson Amendment which prohibits churches and non-profits from engaging in political debate.[21] One of the key players to

---

19 https://www.charismanews.com/opinion/59304-donald-trump-key-to-isaiah-45-prophecy

20 Alveda Kings Take Home Message From Donald Trump – Now Pray! 22 June 2016 https://www.breakingchristiannews.com/articles/display_art.html?ID=18510

21 https://www.drjamesdobson.org/news/commentaries/archives/2016-newsletters/august-newsletter-2016-em?

remove the Johnson Amendment was then House Speaker Paul Ryan. Ryan, a Catholic, said that the only hope for America is a spiritual awakening, and he had sought out pastors for advice, making it a top priority to meet with them. The argument goes that the 1954 Johnson amendment led to the removal of prayer from schools in the early sixties, abortion in the early seventies and the redefining of marriage in 2015, because it had silenced pastors from speaking out on moral and social issues.[22]

The Republican Party itself affirmed that religious freedom in the Bill of Rights protects the right of people to practice their faith in their everyday lives. However, the Democratic Party platform of 2016 stated: *"We support a progressive vision of religious freedom that respects pluralism and rejects the misuse of religion to discriminate."* This is almost a contradiction in terms. Pluralism means diversity yet this progressive vision of diversity would force religious practitioners to align their views with the State. For example, churches would be compelled to compromise their beliefs in the name of equality or diversity or face prosecution. An example of this in Australia was a bill introduced by Federal Labor late in 2018. The changes to the Sex Discrimination Act were introduced to protect school students from being discriminated against on the basis of sexual orientation (even though there have been no recorded cases of this actually occurring.) The Prime Minister, Scott Morrison, said that the effect of the changes proposed by Labor would be that they would stop not only faith-based schools, but all religious bodies, from being able to teach the core beliefs of their faith. Whilst the Prime Minister supported changes to protect

---

sc=FEM&mc=FEM0816NL&utm_source=SilverpopMailing&utm_campaign=201 60804%20Newsletter%20%28FEM0816NL %29%20%282%29&spMailingID=15118639&spUserID=Mjg4MDQ1MTA3Mjgy S0&spJobID=840300197&spReportId=ODQwMzAwMTk3S0

22 What CNN & Fox Won't Tell You About The Move Of God, 8th Aug 2016, https://www.charismanews.com/opinion/59337-what-cnn-and-fox-won-t-tell-you-about-the-move-of-god

children from being discriminated against, he said the changes had to also protect the *"fundamental right to freedom of religion."* [23] At the time of writing, the proposed bill had been referred to a committee.

Jedidiah Morse, the father of American geography, said in 1799 that once a nation overthrows, or neglects the Christian faith, which had given it political and civil freedom, everyone's freedoms would be diminished, and this would lead to despotism. This is what socialism and communism have done, for example, in countries such as North Korea, or the former Union of Soviet Socialist Republics, modern day Russia. Trump however, said he would remove the restriction of the Johnson Amendment and said, *"without religious liberty you don't have liberty."*[24]

Dr James Dobson attended an event called A Conversation with Donald Trump in June 2016, with one thousand other religious leaders. Thirty leaders met with Trump before the meeting and Dobson asked Trump his concerns about religious liberty. Dobson was encouraged that Trump promised to protect religious liberties and felt that his list of potential Supreme Court nominees was *"stellar."* He added, *"We must pray that, if elected, he will keep his word."*[25]

Was Trump courting a religious vote to get himself elected? Dr Lance Wallnau met with Donald Trump and other church leaders in 2015. Here Trump said that the nation had turned against the church in the past decade. During the Obama Administration, Christians in particular had been targeted, sued and forced to resign from jobs because they believed in traditional marriage, wouldn't provide services for

---

23 https://ausprayernet.org.au/a-letter-from-the-prime-minister-concerning-our-religious-liberties/?fbclid=IwAR1l-FqJ8kanFuVGlcEmxlR3GdxdIE1VSZhvGSB1TrYFYYI5YZvjqlEmC1A

24 Trump Meets With Christian Leaders: Without Religious Liberty You Don't Have Liberty, 12 Aug 2016
https://www.breakingchristiannews.com/articles/display_art.html?ID=18928

25 http://www.christianitytoday.com/ct/2016/october/james-dobson-why-i-am-voting-for-donald-trump.html

a same sex wedding or even for preaching a sermon deemed not politically correct.[26] A State Chapter leader of the ACLU (American Civil Liberties Union) resigned her position after her daughters were confronted by biological males in the female toilets. The Obama Administration was directing schools to adopt its transgender policy and to allow students to use the change room of their choice if the student said they identified as the opposite gender. No questions asked, to ask was considered a form of harassment. This led to the ludicrous case of male students claiming to be the opposite gender to get into the girls change rooms to take photos of girls. In another instance, a young girl was allowed to share a room with boys on a school trip because she identified as a boy. Schools were told they must support this policy or lose federal funding.[27] A similar thing has been occurring in Australian schools. The Internal Revenue Service (the U.S. tax department) was exposed for targeting conservative and Christian groups under the Obama Administration, in some cases blocking their tax-exempt status.[28] Organisations that supported the Obama government had their applications processed normally but, those that didn't were processed very, very slowly.[29]

---

26 Cop Accused Of Hatred & Fired For Refusing To Lead Local Gay Parade 27 Feb 2015
https://www.breakingchristiannews.com/articles/display_art.html?ID=15528 and https://www.charismanews.com/politics/issues/56772-oregon-bakers-continue-to-fight-back 27 Apr 2016

27 https://www.lifesitenews.com/blogs/not-just-bathrooms-the-most-dangerous-and-underreported-part-of-obamas-tran

28 IRS Victim Testifies So It Won't Happen To Others, 5 Jun 2013, https://www.breakingchristiannews.com/articles/display_art.html?ID=11724 and – IRS Outed: New Documents Prove Government Agency DID Target Certain Political, Religious Groups, 24 Jul 2015,
https://www.breakingchristiannews.com/articles/display_art.html?ID=16375 and IRS Demanded Content Of Prayers From Pro-Life Group And That's Not All 30 Jul 2015
https://www.breakingchristiannews.com/articles/display_art.html?ID=16407

29 Victory Against IRS Discrimination 8 Aug 2016
https://www.breakingchristiannews.com/articles/display_art.html?ID=18881

Since being elected, Trump has made good on his promises and positive gains have been made for religious liberty. In October 2017 for example, then Attorney General Jeff Sessions issued a memorandum to the Department of Justice, outlining twenty key principles of religious liberty. This included a directive that religious organisations must not be excluded from secular aid programs, and the Internal Revenue Service must not enforce the Johnson Amendment. This means that tax exempt organisations, including churches and religious organisations, are now free to endorse, or oppose, political candidates. The twenty principles also included protection so that individuals would not have to give up religious freedom to participate in the marketplace, or in their interactions with government. And in the spirit of freedom of association, religious organisations are entitled to employ people whose beliefs are consistent with their own.[30] In Australia, political parties are allowed to hire someone who shares their values and 'discriminate' against those who don't. This comes under the banner of freedom of association, meeting together with others who share your values, ethos, beliefs, etc. Yet, there have been some moves to restrict faith-based schools and churches as to whom they can employ. This would make it illegal for them to not hire someone who did not share their values or ethos.

In January 2018 the U.S. Department of Health and Human Services announced it would protect life and an individual's beliefs. It stated that doctors and nurses *"should not be bullied out of the practice of medicine simply because they object to performing abortions against their conscience."* The Office for Civil Rights set up a Conscience and Religious Freedom Division to *"protect individuals and organizations from being compelled to participate in procedures such as abortion, sterilization, and assisted suicide when it would*

---

[30] https://www.lc.org/newsroom/details/100617-trump-instructs-doj-to-protect-religious-freedom

violate their religious beliefs or moral convictions." [31] Late in 2018, Attorney General Sessions criticised the political culture that had attacked people of faith. Nuns had been ordered to buy contraceptives under the Obama administration. People waiting to be appointed as judges were being asked about their religious convictions by Democratic senators, when the American constitution states that there should be no religious test for public office. And there were people who had been taken to court, such as bakers and florists, for not providing services for same sex weddings. Sessions stated that the Trump administration had gone to court many times to defend religious freedom for Christians, Muslims, Jews and those of other faiths. There had even been seven convictions relating to arson, or threats, against houses of worship.[32] In short, there have been advances on religious liberty from the signing of an executive order for religious freedom, to the establishment of a branch of U.S. Human Services that will protect conscience and religious liberty. This is despite LGBTQI activists urging Congress to scrap some religious rights. The activists have said they *"oppose harmful religious exemptions that allow individuals or entities to discriminate under the guise of religious freedom."*[33]

Before the 2016 election, ninety Generals in the military signed an open letter endorsing candidate Trump. One Admiral said that the claim that Trump does not have the temperament to be Commander-in-Chief is erroneous. Senior military leaders who had met with Trump before the election, privately said Trump listens ninety percent of the time and ask

---

31 https://www.hhs.gov/about/news/2018/01/19/hhs-takes-major-actions-protect-conscience-rights-and-life.html

32   https://ausprayernet.org.au/dangerous-movement-eroding-religious-freedom-in-america

33 President Trumps Firewall Of Faith - https://www.breakingchristiannews.com/articles/m_display_art.html?ID=23474 and https://townhall.com/columnists/davidlimbaugh/2018/05/11/denying-trumps-accomplishments-is-increasingly-irrational-n2479535 and https://mobile.wnd.com/2018/01/congress-gets- urged-to-scrap-religious-rights/

questions ten percent of the time *"which is what a CEO and leader does."* Many other retired military leaders didn't sign the letter but said they would be voting for Trump.[34]

The November 2016 Presidential election came down to two candidates. The Democrats' Hillary Clinton would have been the first female President in American history if elected. Following on from the significance of the first African American President, this would have been a great achievement, all politics aside. The other candidate was the Republicans' Donald Trump, a billionaire businessman who some described as like a bull in a china shop when he spoke, one who was not politically correct, and who had been maligned, mocked and despised by the media (including some conservative media commentators).

Yet both nominees were flawed individuals, and who isn't? Trump's lewd comments about women in 2005, that were leaked to the media in October 2016, a month out from the election, shocked many. His comments about racial groups, at times twisted by the media, offended others. Clinton's slate was tarnished by the Wikileaks email scandal, and the use of an unsecured government email server at her home in breach of the law, allegedly wiping thousands of files from her home computer, along with allegations of accepting donations from nation states that supported terrorism, did not bode well for her. One of the stand out moments that possibly cost Clinton the election, was when she said Trump supporters were a *'basket of deplorables.'* To slander one's opponent in a political race is one thing, to slander many ordinary voters is another.

Evangelist Franklin Graham said Trump's crude comments about women from 2005 could not be defended.

---

34 https://www.breakingisraelnews.com/75281/88-u-s-generals-including-holocaust-survivor-sign-letter-trump-support/ and https://www.nytimes.com/2016/09/07/us/politics/donald-trump-earns-backing-of-nearly-90-military-figures.html and www.breakingchristiannews.com/articles/display_art_pf.html?ID=19146

But, neither could the godless, progressive agenda of President Obama and Hillary Clinton. Graham said the only hope for America was God. He spoke about the sins of America that had saturated the nation, and that Christians had a responsibility to remain engaged in politics. Trump apologised for his past sins. Dr Alveda King, niece of Dr Martin Luther King, wrote that the apology was the first step in correcting a wrong. Trump had moved from saying he does not need forgiveness to saying that he has said and done things that he regrets. He had apologised to his wife, family and the nation.[35] As Franklin Graham noted, the election is not about Trump's behaviour from eleven years ago or Clinton's missing emails, it will be about the Supreme Court and who the next President will appoint to that court. *"Evangelicals are going to have to decide which candidate they trust to nominate men and women to the court who will defend the constitution, and support religious freedom."* [36]

Theologian Wayne Grudem said he found both candidates morally objectionable however, he was going to decide who he voted for, based on their policies. *"Do I agree more with Trump's policies or with Clinton's? It isn't even close."* He said Clinton's policies would seriously damage the United States, perhaps forever.[37] In Australia, the Reverend Tim Costello raised concerns about Trump and the religious right trying to *'morph their political goals into Christian principles.'* Seventy-eight percent of evangelicals were throwing their support behind Trump, while Costello felt that

---

35 Dr Alveda King: America Should Apologize Too 10th Oct 2016
https://www.charismanews.com/politics/elections/60438-dr-alveda-king-america-should-apologize-too

36 Franklin Graham: What We Need To Keep In Mind After Donald Trump's Lewd Remarks https://www.charismanews.com/politics/60435-franklin-graham-what-we-need-to-keep-in-mind-after-donald-trump-s-lewd-remarks

37 Prominent Evangelical Theologian Wayne Grudem Reverses Course, Re-Endorses Trump.
https://www.theblaze.com/news/2016/10/21/prominent-evangelical-theologian-wayne-grudem-reverses-course-re-endorses-trump

socialist Bernie Sanders, one of the Democratic Presidential candidates, would address the needs of the poor more effectively. [38] American Rick Joyner on the other hand, wrote that it is valid and useful to talk about political candidates you support and the shortcomings of the ones you don't. However, to question the faith of those who support a particular candidate you don't, is manipulative and controlling. If we can't listen patiently to others and respect them, then perhaps our position is weak and cannot bear to be challenged.

---

38 Trump & The God Card, Eternity, August 2016

Chapter Three

Manifestations

In a post on the Elijah List in September 2016, Jennifer Eivaz from Harvest Christian Centre in California, observed that there were some sincere prophecies about the next President as well as some 'out there' prophecies. Some were prophesying Trump to win, some Clinton, while others prophesied that either one of them being elected would be a sign of God's judgment on America. Her article addressed the issues of praying for the nations and future generations. God answers a nation's problems through the church. She asked, *"Can you pray for a President you don't like? Can you hear the heart of God for a person you don't agree with?"* [39]

Johnny Enlow, author of The Seven Mountain Prophecy, noted that on the Hebrew calendar, 2016 was a Jubilee year. It was also the seventieth Jubilee year since Israel crossed the Jordan river into the promised land. The number seventy speaks of restoration, and is a multiple of perfection (seven) and completeness (ten). A shofar, or trumpet, was blown to proclaim the new season of liberty, a declaration of the Jubilee. He asked if it was more than coincidence that Trump turned seventy in the seventieth Jubilee year.[40] Interestingly, he was sworn in on the 20th of January 2017, and the following day he was seventy years, seven months and

---

[39] How To Discern Prophetic Words For The Upcoming US Presidential Election, 1 Sep 2016, htttp://elijahlist.com/words/display_word.html?ID=16567

[40] 2016: A True Year of Jubilee, 13 Jan 2016, https://www.elijahlist.com/words/display_word.html?ID=15575

seven days old.[41] Seven is a significant biblical number that can mean completion or spiritual perfection. Triple seven speaks of God. Enlow asked what did Trump have to do with the Year of Jubilee? He writes that it has to be more than a coincidence that a man running for political office, whose surname is Trump, turns 70 years old during the 70th Jubilee Year. Enlow wrote he had not heard from God who the next President would be, and he personally had doubts that it would be Donald Trump. *"If Trump is a trumpet or shofar sound that God is using, then we must follow the Biblical pattern."* [42] What's intriguing about Enlow's comments about Trump being a trumpet, is a prophecy from prophet Kim Clement on the 4th of April 2007, years before Trump announced he would run for the presidency. In this prophecy Clement said that God is going to raise up Trump to be a trumpet. [43]

On a side note, the name Donald means great chief or world ruler. John, Trump's middle name, means God is gracious. Put it all together and we get God's grace being outworked through a great chief commencing in a Jubilee year.

The ACPE's word for 2016 came out of a time of seeking the Lord and meeting together in November 2015. As stated in the last chapter, the ACPE prophesied that 2016 would be a tipping point year. Prophet Cindy Jacobs who sits on the council said they believed that God had spoken to them about the church stepping up to its responsibility to pray and to vote righteously, as voting is not compulsory in America. This was going to determine the outcome. *"The Church must awaken, pray, and act."* Jacobs goes on to say that, while they were not shown who the next President would be, they

---

[41] https://www.charismanews.com/opinion/60976-if-donald-trump-wins-he-will-be-70-years-7-months-and-7-days-old-on-his-first-full-day-in-office

[42] Johnny Enlow 2016: A True Year Of Jubilee

https://www.elijahlist.com/words/display_word.html?ID=15575

[43] Kim Clement 4th April 2007, Redding CA,
https://houseofdestiny.org/prophecy

believed God was saying He was preparing a patriot, and that the church would have to pray earnestly. She added, *"The Lord also spoke that a conservative revolt would shake up the elections and cause even the months leading up to the elections to be tumultuous."* [44]

A conservative revolt. After Trump's election win, a headline in the Herald Sun newspaper said, *"Big Apple Stunned By The Middle Finger To The Establishment."* Columnist Andrew Bolt's headline was, *"It's a revolt against the Left's arrogance."* [45] In fact, the election result was a tipping point and could be fairly said to have been a conservative revolt. The media and the Left by and large did not see it coming. They ignored the crowd numbers turning out at political rallies during the 2016 election campaign. For example, only thirty people, including the media, turned out to hear the Democratic Vice-Presidential candidate Tim Kaine in West Palm Beach, Florida. Meanwhile, twenty thousand attended a Trump rally in Tampa, Florida.[46] They ignored the fact that Trump was getting more people to his rallies, some lining up outside venues for hours.

Over a three-month period between August and October 2016, Hillary Clinton appeared at thirty-four campaign rallies. Of these, approximately a dozen had crowds in excess of one thousand. Trump on the other hand appeared at eighty-seven rallies where seven rallies had less than one thousand people in attendance. Sixteen rallies had crowds in excess of ten thousand and Trump's crowd average was six thousand plus, compared to Clinton's average of less than one

---

44 https://www.generals.org/articles/single/word-of-the-lord-for-2016/

45 Herald Sun 10th November 2016, pg 3 & 9

46 https://www.thegatewaypundit.com/2016/10/wow-tim-kaine-holds-rally-30-people-show/ and https://www.breitbart.com/big-government/2016/10/24/tampa-turns-out-big-for-trump-in-pivotal-swing-florida-county/ and https://www.breakingchristiannews.com/articles/display_art.html?ID=19544

thousand.⁴⁷ A people movement was underway and the media could not, or did not want to, see it.

What the media missed, the church didn't, with many calls to prayer issued during 2015 and 2016 in America. Many Christians mobilised in 2016, with over five hundred pastors standing for political office at local, state and federal levels that year.⁴⁸ Franklin Graham said it was time for the church to be heard. Focus on the Family founder, James Dobson, stated his reasons why he would be voting for Donald Trump, while the Azusa Now and United Cry prayer events attracted tens of thousands who cried out to God for their nation.⁴⁹

During October 2018, large crowds turned out at political rallies for the midterm elections where President Trump spoke. For example, the rally in Houston Texas had to be moved from the NRG Center which could seat eight thousand, to the Toyota Center, which seated eighteen thousand. Dallas News reported that there were sixteen thousand people inside the venue and another ten to fifteen thousand outside. One-hundred-thousand people had asked for tickets. People camped out the previous day, some arriving up to thirty-two hours before the event commenced. There was a similar scene in Montana, with supporters arriving before dawn, lining up in the cold for the evening rally. In some places, cars were abandoned on the side of the road miles from the venue with occupants walking the rest of the distance. In several states where early voting commenced, NBC News

---

47 https://www.thegatewaypundit.com/2016/10/no-joke-hillary-rarely-has-more-than-1000-at-her-events

48 Good News: Hundreds Of Inspired Christians Are Running For Office, 8 Jun 2016,
https://www.breakingchristiannews.com/articles/display_art.html?ID=18390 and https://www.reuters.com/article/us-usa-election-evangelicals-idUSKBN0TU16M20151211 and https://pjmedia.com/faith/2016/1/7/over-500-pastors-will-run-for-office-in-2016/

49 www.breakingchristiannews.com/articles/display_art.html?ID=17977 and www.breakingchristiannews.com/articles/display_art.html?ID=17996 and
www.breakingchristiannews.com/articles/display_art.html?ID=18563 and www.breakingchristiannews.com/articles/display_art.html?ID=19371

noted that Republican voters outnumbered Democratic voters in seven out of eight states.[50] The people attending these rallies were peaceful too, even though there were some who were peddling goods to attendees that were not always polite or appropriate. The people movement from 2016 showed no signs of abating.

Dr Lance Wallnau is an internationally recognised speaker and business and political strategist. Before the 2016 election, Wallnau said, *"If history tells us anything it's this – when God shows up, He's disguised and His people don't always recognise Him."*[51] Wallnau met with other Christian leaders and Donald Trump in December 2015. Trump said to them that America had a long period of Christian consensus, but now every other ideological group had a voice while the church had become soft. He believed Christians had become a people living in fear, and while Christians likely made up the single largest constituency, they had no unity and no punch.[52] He also said that America had turned against the church in the past decade.

Wallnau writes that back in 2015, he believed the Lord spoke to him and said Donald Trump would be the wrecking ball to the spirit of political correctness. He noted that the Progressive agenda is being driven by a demonic spirit that is committed to *"your conversion or eradication."* He also noted that no political candidate in history had *"ever stirred up so*

---

50 https://www.dallasnews.com/news/politics/2018/10/22/die-hards-camp-spots-donald-trump-ted-cruz-rally-houston and https://www.redstate.com/brandon_morse/2018/10/23/media-hides-laughable-turnout-obamas-nevada-speech-trumpcruz-houston-rally-saw-thousands-attendance/ and https://www.thegatewaypundit.com/2018/10/jaw-dropping-thousands-line-up-in-cold-for-President-trump-rally-in-missoula-montana-photos-and-video/ and https://www.nytimes.com/2018/10/22/us/trump-rally-texas-houston-scene.html and https://www.newser.com/story/266274/texas-sees-massive-turnout-in-early-voting.html

51 An Interview With Dr Lance Wallnau by Steve Strang, 5 Oct 2016 https://www.elijahlist.com/words/display_word.html?ID=16740

52 https://www.charismanews.com/opinion/59304-donald-trump-key-to-isaiah-45-prophecy

many devils at one time". He predicted that the Left would manifest, and we have certainly seen that from the street protests with placards proclaiming f*** Trump, to the calls for resistance from political leaders like Hillary Clinton. The media coverage of Trump has been predominantly negative as well. Wallnau expected the craziness to go to another level and Trump would be blamed.

That was Wallnau's prediction before the 2016 election. How does it stand up post November 2016? Here's just a snapshot of what has transpired in the two years since Trump was elected. Two days after he was sworn in as President in January 2017, a large Women's March was held in Washington DC. At this event, singer Madonna spoke of blowing up the White House, actress Sarah Silverman called for a military coup to depose the newly elected President, while actress Ashley Judd claimed she could feel Hitler in the streets, and claimed that members of Trump's cabinet were Nazis.[53]

Let's just pick up on the Nazi claim for a moment. Adolf Hitler was a socialist, the word Nazi being an acronym for National Socialist German Workers Party. Trump is not a socialist. Hitler hated the Jews. Trump has a Jewish son-in-law, has promised to stand by Israel unlike his predecessor, moved the U.S. embassy to Jerusalem, has had a coin minted in Israel with his face on it, and has been endorsed by Israel's Prime Minister. The Nazis put Gestapo agents in church services to spy on them and to make sure the churches complied with government directives such as, what kind of prayers they could pray. Trump has spoken often about Christianity being under attack both at home and abroad, and promised to defend the Christian faith. Around half of his

---

53　https://townhall.com/tipsheet/christinerousselle/2017/02/02/no-big-deal-or-anything-but-sarah-silverman-just-called-for-a-coup-to-overthrow-the-government-n2280291 and https://www.dailymail.co.uk/news/article-4142950/Thousands-women-head-Washington-protest-Trump.html and https://variety.com/2017/biz/news/ashley-judd-nasty-woman-womens-march-video-watch-1201966160/

cabinet are people of faith.[54] (Psalm 1 – blessed is the man who does not walk in the counsel of the wicked.) Hitler hated black skinned people. Trump has Dr Ben Carson, an African American on his team, and the first African American judge to swear in a Vice President was present at the inauguration. The Nazis expected everyone to serve, and die for, the Fuhrer and the State. Trump said in his inauguration address that the nation exists to serve its citizens. He also said, the Bible tells us how good and pleasant it is when God's people live together in unity, that America was protected by God, and all children are infused with the breath of life by the same almighty Creator.[55] The ironic thing is that the labelling of Trump, conservatives and Christians as Nazis (i.e. national socialists) comes from some who embrace socialism. The conclusion one draws from this is that, according to these socialists, socialism must be bad for you, and therefore they themselves must be bad. Or perhaps they are complimenting you because you are the same as them? Or perhaps they are quite ignorant and naïve because they have no clue that the acronym, Nazi, includes the word socialist.

It is interesting that the cries of *"Not my President"*, *"<bleep> Donald Trump"* and *"<bleep> white people,"* come from people who claim to be inclusive and tolerant, and who believe that love trumps hate. I suppose it depends on one's definition of love. During the Vietnam War era the catch cry was 'make love not war.' This was also the time of anti-war protests and, in the U.S., violent riots. It was a time of hippies, people experimenting with drugs and embracing sexual promiscuity, or *"free love"* as it was called. It was also a time of anti-military sentiment in Australia that saw protests at Anzac Day marches. 'Make love not war' and 'Love trumps

---

54 https://www.breakingchristiannews.com/articles/display_art.html?ID=20210

55 https://www.whitehouse.gov/briefings-statements/the-inaugural-address/

hate' all seem to be birds of the same feather. Interestingly, tolerance was once understood to mean the opposite of acceptance. We don't tolerate something that we admire but, rather, we tolerate what we dislike. Think about that for a moment. Tolerance is not *"an imperative of love but a restraint of one's hatred."*[56]

Hollywood actress Zoe Saldana, who stars in the new Star Trek movies, said that Hollywood's treatment of the President was arrogant and bullying.[57] Broadway star Carole Cook asked where John Wilkes Booth (the man who assassinated Lincoln) is when you need him? Democratic Congresswoman Maxine Waters called for people to harass those who worked for the Trump administration. She said, *"If you see anybody from that cabinet in a restaurant, in a department store, at a gasoline station, you get out and you create a crowd. And you push back on them. Tell them they're not welcome any more, anywhere."* One could almost draw a comparison to the tactics of the Klu Klux Klan implementing similar actions outside the homes of African Americans last century. This is ironic given that Waters is African American. Trump officials have since been feeling the heat. Press Secretary Sarah Huckabee-Sanders was asked to leave a restaurant two minutes after arriving. Her response to that was that it said more about the owner of the restaurant than her. *"I always do my best to treat people, including those I disagree with, respectfully and will continue to do so."*[58] Several others have been harassed with protests outside restaurants, confrontations while dining out, and protests outside their

---

[56] In Defence Of Freedom Of Speech, Chris Berg, Institute of Public Affairs, 2012 pg 42.

[57] https://www.breakingchristiannews.com/articles/display_art.html?ID=20263

[58] https://townhall.com/tipsheet/timothymeads/2018/06/23/sarah-huckabee-sanders-gracefully-responds-to-va-restaurant-that-refused-her-service-n2493765 and https://www.lifesitenews.com/blogs/democratic-congresswoman-we-must-turn-on...harass-trump-officials-at-gas-st 25 June 2018 and

https://edition.cnn.com/2018/06/25/politics/maxine-waters-trump-officials/index.html

homes. Another person was even asked to leave a restaurant, while another had their car rammed because of a pro-Trump bumper sticker.[59] A letter laced with poison Ricin was sent to James Mattis, the Secretary for Defence, while the office of Senator Ted Cruz received letters containing white powder.[60] Donald Trump Jr was also sent a letter containing white powder early in 2018.[61] And in September 2018 a man was jailed after shouting obscenities, threatening, and then trying to stab a Republican congressional candidate.[62]

During 2018 the manifestations didn't cease. Actor Robert De Niro, before he introduced Bruce Springsteen at the Tony Awards in June said, *"It's no longer down with Trump. It's f*** Trump,"* to which he received a standing ovation from the celebrity audience.[63] Isn't that a form of hate speech? Or does that only apply to people we don't like saying it? Former Democrat Attorney General Eric Holder said it was time to kick Republicans.[64] Prominent U.S. TV host, Bill Maher, said he was hoping the economy would collapse, as that would be the only way to get rid of Trump.[65] Evangelist Franklin Graham's response to that comment was, it showed the liberal Left to be vicious. He called on Christians to pray that the President doesn't fail, to ask God to help and for Trump to succeed for the good of the nation.[66]

---

59 https://www.usatoday.com/story/news/politics/onpolitics/2018/08/02/trump-bumper-sticker-enraged-driver/893265002/

60 https://townhall.com/tipsheet/mattvespa/2018/10/24/hillary-clinton-on-bomb-threats-we-need-to-come-togetherafter-i-said-that-we-cant-be-civil-with-republicans-n2531551

61 https://www.bbc.com/news/world-us-canada-43034789

62 https://www.heraldsun.com.au/blogs/andrew-bolt/republican-attacked-by-leftist-knifeman/news-story/c770a99be64c421ef226e5fb76439af4

63 https://variety.com/2018/legit/news/robert-de-niro-trump-tonys-1202839957/

64 https://townhall.com/tipsheet/mattvespa/2018/10/24/hillary-clinton-on-bomb-threats-we-need-to-come-togetherafter-i-said-that-we-cant-be-civil-with-republicans-n2531551

65 https://www.washingtonexaminer.com/news/bill-maher-is-hoping-for-an-economic-collapse-so-he-can-get-rid-of-trump-sorry-if-that-hurts-people

66 http://www.breakingchristiannews.com/articles/m_display_art.html?

During the Supreme Court nomination process from July to October 2018, thousands of protestors opposed to Trump's court nominee Brett Kavanaugh, descended on Washington DC. Their protests were loud and noisy, something I encountered during a pro-life march in Melbourne in 2012. Whilst I was 'on the job' for the Christian radio station I was employed with at the time, to try and get views from both sides, the radical pro-choice protestors made a lot of noise, banging on drums, name calling and using foul language (such as f*** off bigots.) This revealed their tactics were more about bullying those with a different opinion.

Republican Steve Scalise survived a politically motivated assassination attempt after being shot at baseball practice in July 2017, by a lone Bernie Sanders (Democrat) supporter. Senator Rand Paul witnessed the shooting of Steve Scalise and others at that practice match. Paul's wife Kelley wrote an open letter to Democratic senator Cory Booker, calling on him to retract his statement to encourage people to *"get up in the face"* of those they didn't agree with. She said for the previous eighteen months her family had *"experienced violence and threats of violence at a horrifying level."* There were now regular police patrols in their street, especially after a Democratic staffer published personal details of Republican politicians online. That staff member was soon arrested.[67] Kelley Paul also wrote about the physical injuries her husband sustained in November 2017, when he was physically assaulted in their yard, sustaining six broken ribs, lung damage and recurring pneumonia. Singers Cher and Bette Midler praised the attack, while an MSNBC news commentator said that event was one of her 'favourite' stories. Kelley said she now keeps a loaded gun by her bed.[68] The chairperson for the

---

ID=24761

67 https://www.washingtonexaminer.com/news/us-capitol-police-arrest-suspect-behind-doxing-of-at-least-one-senator

68 https://edition.cnn.com/2018/10/03/opinions/rand-paul-suffer-intimidation-and-threats-kelley-paul/index.html?no-st=1538613026 and https://www.courier-journal.com/story/news/politics/2018/02/10/bette-midler-

Republicans in Minnesota claimed that she had received numerous death threats, while two Republican candidates had been assaulted in what was thought to be politically motivated violence.[69]

In an interview with CNN on the 9th of October 2018, Hillary Clinton said that America was dealing with an ideological party that had a lust for power, and therefore, Democrats needed to be tougher. The time to be civil, would be when the Democrats had taken back control of the House or the Senate.[70] That type of statement has a Machiavellian flavor to it – the end justifies the means. How civil though is civil? One Democrat, newly elected in the 2018 midterm elections, speaking about Trump said she wanted to *"impeach the mother f*******.[71] Two weeks after the CNN interview, the Clintons, along with former President Obama, leftist billionaire George Soros, a number of other Democrats including Maxine Waters and actor Robert De Niro, had suspicious packages delivered to their homes, or intercepted by the Secret Service. These were identified as pipe bombs and fortunately no one was killed. Many Republican leaders were quick to condemn the homemade bombs, and Trump said the full weight of the government would be deployed to find out who did it.[72] The Left were quick to point the blame at Trump's rhetoric, while the Right were quick to say it smells like a set up to influence the November midterms. Many

---

tweets-rand-paul-attack/325701002/

69   https://freebeacon.com/politics/two-gop-candidates-assaulted-minnesota/

70   https://www.usatoday.com/story/news/politics/onpolitics/2018/10/09/hillary-clinton-cnn-interview/1578636002/

71   https://www.theguardian.com/us-news/2019/jan/04/democrats-congress-trump-impeach-rashida-tlaib and
https://edition.cnn.com/2019/01/04/politics/rashida-tlaib-trump-impeachment-comments/index.html

72   https://townhall.com/tipsheet/katiepavlich/2018/10/24/republicans-strongly-condemn-package-bomb-attacks-on-democrats-n2531557

Democratic leaders also condemned the bombs, and rightly so, including Hillary Clinton, who said it was a troubling time and people needed to bring the country together.[73] This is in stark contrast to her statement two weeks earlier that this was no time to be civil.

Actor Peter Fonda tweeted in the middle of 2018, that young Baron Trump should be taken from his mother's arms and put in a cage with pedophiles, to see if his mother would stand up to the giant <bleep> she is married to.[74] Fonda later apologised for the tweet.[75] In addition, during October 2018, Republican offices in Florida, North Carolina, Wyoming, California, Arizona, Illinois, Kentucky, Nebraska and New York were targeted. They were shot at, vandalised, firebombed, spray painted with words like "Nazi Republicans leave town or else", or "Rape" (referring to the Kavanaugh confirmation). They had been set on fire, rocks had been thrown through windows and a small truck was set alight.[76]

Fox News host Sean Hannity, listed a string of attacks against Republicans during a broadcast on 26th October 2018. These included Republican Senator Mitch McConnell being harassed while dining out at a restaurant and at an airport; a New York man being charged with threatening two Republican senators, two Republican candidates being physically assaulted and the son of a Republican senator, was also assaulted. The Democrats' Eric Holder was telling activists *'we kick 'em.'* A Republican senator's wife was sent a beheading video because of her husband's support for judge

---

73 https://nypost.com/2018/10/24/hillary-responds-to-spate-of-package-bombs-its-a-troubling-time-in-america/
74 http://www.foxnews.com/entertainment/2018/06/20/peter-fonda-tweets-wants-to-rip-barron-trump-from-his-mother-and-put-him-in-cage-with-pedophiles.html
75 https://www.huffingtonpost.com.au/entry/peter-fonda-barron-trump_us_5b2b6bb1e4b0040e273fba5a
76 They're Democrats: Shots Fired at Volusia GOP HQ
https://townhall.com/tipsheet/mattvespa/2018/10/29/sAots-fired-at-volusia-gop-hq-n2532994

Kavanaugh, while other Republicans had received death threats over the Kavanaugh issue. And that was for the first three weeks of October 2018.[77] The list went back further but I think you get my point. Yet the media's big story for October wasn't about the number of Republican offices vandalised or the attacks against Republican senators. It was about the lone pipe bomber, allegedly a Trump supporter, who targeted high profile Democrats. The media blamed it on Trump and his rhetoric. All acts of violence, regardless of which side, should be condemned by the media and politicians, yet it does not always seem to be this way.

In April 2019, a petition was started, calling on Facebook and Twitter to suspend Trump from their platforms, citing his 'hate speech' as their concern. This was in response to Trump tweeting a video of one of the House Democrats saying that 9/11 was *"some people did something,"* with footage of that terrible day. All he tweeted was *"we will never forget"* and video of her words with scenes of the towers on fire, yet his reference to her words was labelled as hate speech by some. The Democrat concerned has received death threats for what she said, which is unequivocally wrong, yet as Lance Wallnau said, Trump will get the blame.[78] It's sad that in our day and age, hate has been dumbed down to mean disagreement. It's worrying that social media giants are seeing it that way and suspending views they disagree with.

I believe we are witnessing what the Bible says, that our battle is not against flesh and blood but against principalities, powers and spiritual wickedness. That doesn't mean that the people saying and doing these things are demon possessed or intentionally evil, but rather, the influence they are under is darkly spiritual, whether they know it or not or

---

[77] https://www.youtube.com/watch?v=rt4w4Cn6oqs accessed 4 April 2019

[78] https://townhall.com/tipsheet/bethbaumann/2019/04/13/i-sdems-hypocrisy-soars-to-new-highs-when-they-refuse-to-say-9-11-was-committed-n2544736 and https://actionnetwork.org/petitions/suspend-trump-from-facebook-and-twitter

believe it or not. And that can happen to anyone, even Christians. There but for the grace of God go I.

Wallnau's prediction about the 'Left manifesting' and the craziness going to a whole new level has been spot on. Wallnau believed that Trump brought courage, he had backbone and was willing to voice his opinion. We've seen even in our own nation how political correctness has been twisting words and demonising people, keeping many, including church leaders, quiet for fear of offending or lawsuits. The Catch the Fire Ministries, or the two Dannys case, in Victoria in 2005, is an example of what happens when one does not comply with political correctness. Political correctness is under the influence of a Leviathan spirit, which is like a giant crocodile or python, that twists and suffocates its prey. Wallnau observed that once Trump stepped into the room, he collided with the PC crowd.

He also believed that Trump was a 'common grace' candidate. The term 'common grace' is a theological term that is used to describe the grace of God working through secular individuals and institutions, to prevent *'society from imploding.'* Some of the 2016 Republican presidential candidates, such as Ted Cruz and Ben Carson, were Christians, just like Salmon P Chase, a devout evangelical who stood for the ballot in 1860 against Abraham Lincoln. Some church leaders back then considered Lincoln to be a godless sceptic because he was not a regular church attender.[79] Yet history has shown that Lincoln was the right man, for the right job, at the right time.

Another point of interest that Wallnau observed before the election, was that Donald Trump would be the 45th President of the United States. After the meeting with Trump, Wallnau believed he was led of the Lord to read Isaiah 45. He said that, when he met Trump, he sensed there was an anointing on him which he did not understand at that meeting.

---

[79] God's Chaos Candidate, Dr Lance Wallnau, Killer Sheep Media Inc, 2016, pgs 63-71

This almost contradicted a theology that said only godly people can be anointed. Wallnau stated he actually preferred other candidates such as Ted Cruz, Marco Rubio and Carly Fiorina.[80] After he saw on Facebook that Trump would be the 45th President if elected, he turned to Isaiah 45.

This chapter is a prophecy about a secular leader, King Cyrus, God was going to raise up and anoint. God called Cyrus his anointed, meaning, a secular king was anointed by the Lord! What this secular gentile king did, was to end a period of spiritual captivity and decline, which brought about the end of Jeremiah's seventy years of captivity prophecy. Cyrus also gave a decree to restore and rebuild Jerusalem.[81]

As Wallnau began to research King Cyrus, he discovered that an archaeological dig in 1879 uncovered an object that has been called the Cyrus cylinder. This cylinder was dated back to the time of the Old Testament prophet Daniel, and a portion of the cylinder was dictated by Cyrus himself. There are three things mentioned on this cylinder. Cyrus dealt with terror, restored economic stability and he honoured the Jewish houses of faith. Wallnau noted that these three things, terrorism, the economy and faith, were issues that Trump said he was going to deal with, if elected.[82]

In December 2017, Trump announced that America would move its Israeli embassy from Tel Aviv to Jerusalem, recognising that city as the Jewish capital. In May 2018 an Israeli organisation minted a coin depicting King Cyrus and Donald Trump. Cyrus allowed the Jews to return from exile in Babylon to Jerusalem to rebuild their temple, and Trump's decision to move the American embassy to Jerusalem in May 2018, came on the seventieth anniversary of modern Israel's

---

[80] https://www.charismanews.com/opinion/60395-why-christians-aren-t-laughing-at-lance-wallnau-saying-god-is-raising-up-donald-trump-like-cyrus-in-isaiah-45

[81] https://www.charismanews.com/opinion/59304-donald-trump-key-to-isaiah-45-prophecy

[82] https://www.elijahlist.com/words/display_word.html?ID=16740

founding.[83] Coincidence, or fulfilment of Wallnau's prophetic prediction?

No one has prophesied that Donald Trump will be a refined, upstanding, gentleman. The media, and the politically correct, like to preach that everyone should be perfect or that politicians should be dignified or befitting for the role! However, what the prophecies are indicating is that this man has been anointed by God to bring about changes in a nation that has fallen away from the Christian values it was founded on. God has chosen this man, warts and all, to accomplish His purposes in America. Evangelical leader Franklin Graham was asked how he could defend Trump when he had done some decadent things in his life. Graham's response was that he had, *"never said he was the best example of the Christian faith. He defends the faith. And I appreciated that very much."* He noted that Trump had apologised for his past ways to his wife and daughter, and like all of us, will have to give an account before God for the way he has lived his life.[84]

Our duty as believers is to pray FOR those in authority as Paul writes to Timothy. Pray for our political leaders, not only the ones we would vote for, but also for those we would not. Why don't you take a moment right now to pray for your local member of parliament and for the Prime Minister, or your state Premier, and opposition leaders. This is ministry in the opposite spirit. It restricts the powers of darkness and releases God's access to those positions of authority. Remember, whatever we bind on earth is bound in heaven, and whatever we loose on earth is loosed in heaven.

---

83 https://www.alaraby.co.uk/english/News/2018/5/13/Trumps-face-to-feature-on-newly-minted-Israeli-coin and

https://abcnews.go.com/International/israeli-group-sells-special-edition-trump-coin/story?id=55096698

84 Franklin Graham: I Back Trump Because He Defends Christian faith. https://www.newsmax.com/newsfront/franklin-graham-trump-christians/2018/11/26/id/891944/

Chapter Four

The 2007 Prophecy

The late Kim Clement, a South African who emigrated to the United States and became a prophet to that nation, has a very positive track record with prophetic words that have come to pass. His accuracy in prophesying events such as 9/11, (a prophecy given in 1996), the hiding places of Osama bin Laden and Saddam Hussein, warnings about terrorist attacks, the emergence of ISIS, weather events like Hurricane Katrina in 2005, and who would be elected President of the United States (he prophesied Bush, Obama and Trump), is amazing. The focus of the next chapters will be about the prophecies Clement made regarding the forty-fifth President of the United States.

On February 10th 2007, more than nine years before the 2016 election, Clement prophesied about a future President for America. The key points from this prophecy were: -

- God would place a man at the helm for two terms.
- He would be a praying President, not a religious one.
- God said He (that is God) is going to fool the people.
- The future President would be described as having 'hot blood'.
- This President would bring the walls of protection on the country and the economy would change rapidly.

- This President will be baptised in the Holy Spirit once in office.[85]

As mentioned in chapter 3, in April 2007, Clement prophesied that God said He would raise up Donald Trump to be a trumpet. On the 27th of July 2007, he prophesied that once again there would be a man of Irish descent in the White House. (The other man of Irish descent was a reference to President John F. Kennedy.) This future man of Irish descent would be in the years to come, and he would be one with uprightness, morality and great strength of leadership. At first glance, this seems to contradict the February prophecy however, as stated in Chapter One, three old testament prophecies about Jesus seemed to contradict each other as well. The July prophecy is significant because it ties into the February prophecy. Mike Pence is Trump's Vice President, and Pence said his Irish grandfather was a big influence on his life. [86]

Here we see the emergence of the man of Irish descent at the time of Trump becoming President. Pence is also a Christian, and was attacked by some voices in the media because he said he would never eat alone with another woman (other than his wife), and that he would never go to an event where alcohol was being served, unless his wife was present. According to the PC narrative, this made him some kind of sexist, misogynist, bigot.[87] This smearing of Pence occurred just before the alleged immoral sexual misdeeds of Hollywood mogul, Harvey Weinstein, made the news. Weinstein at the time of writing was awaiting trial and denies the allegations. However, what was alleged was perhaps an example of what real misogyny and sexism looks like. Pence had put

---

85 Kim Clement, 10th February 2007, www.houseofdestiny.org/prophecy

86 Kim Clement, 27th July 2007. www.houseofdestiny.org/prophecy and https://www.irishcentral.com/news/mike-pence-the-next-irish-american-President-82776907-237682561

87 https://www1.cbn.com/cbnnews/politics/2017/march/pence-marriage-rule-wise-advice-or-misogynistic-throwback

boundaries in place to protect himself, and to honor his wife and their marriage. Those boundaries at first glance in the 21st century might seem old fashioned, but values of fidelity, honour, love and commitment have stood the test of time.

In 2016 we saw the convergence of three prophetic words from 2007 – God raising up Trump to be a trumpet, the man of Irish descent being placed in the White House and the President with 'hot blood' who would restore the economy and protect the nation. There are four key points from this February 2007 prophecy I wish to highlight.

Point #1: God said he would fool the people. How shocked was the world when Trump was declared the winner of the election? How shocked were you? How shocked was the media? If you do a search on Google for Media Fails, Donald Trump Can't Win, or Media Meltdown Election Night, you will find media personalities mocking and ridiculing that Trump could become President, or in shock as the final results came through on election night. This prophecy states there would be a man who would be President for two terms. Connect that to the economy changing rapidly and building a wall to protect the nation and perhaps the shock is not yet over!

Point # 2: The next point in the prophecy is about a praying President, *"not a religious one."* Trump has met with church leaders many times and has allowed them to pray for him on numerous occasions. This was reported in 2017, for example, by the Christian network CBN News, [88] the Washington Post [89], Christianity Today [90] and the PBS News Hour. [91] Could this be connected to the prophecy? This is not a

---

[88] https://www1.cbn.com/cbnnews/us/2017/july/faith-leaders-enjoy-open-door-at-white-house

[89] https://www.washingtonpost.com/news/acts-of-faith/wp/2017/07/12/photo-surfaces-of-evangelical-pastors-laying-hands-on-trump-in-the-oval-office/?noredirect=on&utm_term=.c0ebbb45c5b7

[90] https://www.christianitytoday.com/ct/2017/may-web-only/precarious-task-of-praying-with-Presidents-in-media-age.html

[91] https://www.youtube.com/watch?v=QKlk443i7ag

judgment on whether or not Trump is a born-again Christian, however what has been clear since before he was elected, and after he was elected, is that he stands up for, and defends, the Christian faith. Not all Christians in America voted for him, although it was an overwhelming large percentage of the evangelical vote that helped to elect him in 2016. Various American church leaders during 2015 and 2016 began to speak out, and called the church to pray in the lead up to the elections. They challenged Christians to consider who would be appointed to the U.S. Supreme Court under the next President.

I've heard it said that when it comes to electing politicians, we Christians need to consider (i) our biblical values; (ii) what political party's values line up closest to these; and (iii) who will stand up for those values if elected. We will likely never find a politician whose values will totally line up with ours and, if we do, they may not line up with the person of faith standing next to us. In the past I was always encouraged to hear that such and such a politician was a Christian, but now I think it's more important that the person is anointed for the task, whether or not they are a believer. But I digress.

Point # 3: The next point is about the economy changing rapidly. The following news highlights about the economy changes, in just under two years under Trump's presidency, reveal positive gains. Company tax cuts passed in December 2017 were dismissed by the media, and the Democrats, as favouring the rich. There was criticism of the bonuses for workers, calling them crumbs, and that it would be akin to the end of the world. Meanwhile, approximately 80% of taxpayers would go on to benefit from the cuts. Consumer confidence and the stock market reached record highs,[92] while

---

[92] https://townhall.com/tipsheet/mattvespa/2017/12/24/watch-cbs-news-finds-three-families-who-will-be-getting-serious-relief-thanks-to-trumps-tax-cuts-n2426404/

one State governor called the tax cuts *'evil in the extreme.'*[93] An opinion piece in the Sydney Morning Herald, claimed that Trump's proposed company tax cuts would not work, they would reduce economic activity and no more people would be employed.[94]

CBS News spoke to three families from the single mum on $40K to the couple on $300K. All said they would be better off, even though they originally believed they wouldn't be.[95] In fact, almost 880,000 people became millionaires in the first twelve months after the tax cuts were introduced.[96] That means there was actually more wealth being spread across the population.

The black unemployment rate is at its lowest level in history despite claims Trump is a racist.[97] An opinion poll published by Rasmussen Reports in August 2018, showed that Trump's approval rating with African Americans has catapulted from 8% in 2016, to 36% in 2018.[98] Unemployment is also down for other minority groups, while hourly rates for workers are up.[99] Since the tax cuts, hundreds of companies have handed out bonuses of between $1000 to $3000 to their employees, and many companies increased philanthropic

---

[93] https://www.mercurynews.com/2017/12/04/jerry-brown-tax-plan-gop-congress/

[94] https://www.smh.com.au/business/why-President-trumps-tax-cuts-wont-fire-up-the-us-economy-20170929-gyr9lw.html

[95] https://www.realclearpolitics.com/video/2017/12/22/cbs_how_will_tax_cuts_affect_your_family.html

[96] https://www.washingtonexaminer.com/washington-secrets/america-first-878-000-millionaires-added-in-last-12-months-trump-effect-relentless

[97] https://townhall.com/tipsheet/guybenson/2018/01/05/jobs-report-n2430642

[98] https://www.usatoday.com/story/news/politics/onpolitics/2018/08/16/trump-approval-rating-african-americans-rasmussen-poll/1013212002/

[99] https://www.breakingchristiannews.com/articles/m_display_art.html?ID=24687

activity.[100] According to one article I came across whilst researching for this book, during Obama's first nineteen months in office, 4.4 million people lost their jobs. During Trump's first nineteen months in office, 3.5 million people had been employed. Since the turn of this century, over twenty percent of jobs growth in the United States has occurred since Trump became President. That's twenty percent in less than two years, which is an amazing result. Black business ownership was also up a whopping four hundred percent in twelve months.[101]

Because of the tax cuts, U.S. companies with offshore operations are bringing more money back into the country. For the first quarter of 2017, $38 billion was brought back into the country. For the first quarter of 2018, that figure was over $300 billion![102] At the end of July 2018, 4.1% growth in the economy was announced, while the trade deficit had dropped by more than $50 billion. This was contrary to claims before the 2016 election by Clinton, Obama and national economists, that Trump would bring recession, and his claim of 4.0% growth would not be achievable. CNN Money quoted economists as saying Trump's promise of 4.0% growth would not happen. The Los Angeles Times said, if Trump thinks he can get 3.0% growth, he's dreaming. The Wall Street Journal said the growth Trump was promising was out of reach, while President Obama wanted to know if Trump had a magic wand.[103] Yet less than two years after becoming President, Trump's "dreaming" of 4.0% growth had been achieved.

---

100 https://townhall.com/tipsheet/mattvespa/2018/06/05/good-news-the-booming-trump-economy-looks-unstoppable-n2487536 and
https://townhall.com/tipsheet/mattvespa/2018/01/15/boom-over-two-million-workers-have-received-bonuses-and-raises-thanks-to-trumps-n2434777
101 https://townhall.com/columnists/wayneallynroot/2018/09/11/trump-the-worst-racist-of-all-time-n2517589
102 https://www.foxbusiness.com/markets/american-money-is-flowing-back-into-america
103 https://mobile.wnd.com/2018/07/flashback-dems-warned-trump-would-tank-economy/ and http://www.foxnews.com/politics/2018/07/27/gdp-report-shows-booming-4-1-percent-growth-as-trump-touts-terrific-numbers.html

Maybe he did have a 'magic wand' after all?

During 2017, the stock market hit all-time highs eighty-five times. (More about the stock market in chapter 5.) There was over six trillion dollars more in the stock market and twenty-two red tape regulations had been cut for everyone introduced. [104] The cutting of red tape saves money, something the Australian Institute for Public Affairs is quick to point out, claiming it costs the Australian economy $176 billion each year.[105] For the first time since 2003, American beef imports returned to China, opening up a $2.5 billion market to American ranchers and producers.[106] Under Obama, recipients of welfare ballooned but, under Trump, millions of Americans had dropped their Food Stamp enrolment, meaning they were coming off welfare.[107] On the 26th of October 2018, the White House released a briefing showing that in more than half the states of America, unemployment was at record low rates and / or jobs growth was up. Headings for the different states included *"lowest point in nearly thirty years"*, *"unemployment falls to record lows"* and *"jobs reach all time high."*[108] These appear to be considerable economic achievements and perhaps the beginning of fulfilling this prophetic word given in 2007.

Clement also gave other prophetic words regarding the U.S. economy. For example, on the 18th of February 2011, he prophesied regarding those who would say there would be national socialism in America, and how they planned to create history without God. But God said He would make history.

---

104 Remarks by President Trump on the Administrations National Security Strategy, 18 Dec 2017, https://www.White House.gov/briefings-statements/remarks-President-trump-administrations-national-security-strategy/

105 https://ipa.org.au/red-tape-project

106 Trump restores military's focus on mission, point # 108 http://www.wnd.com/2017/11/4621979/

107 https://townhall.com/tipsheet/katiepavlich/2018/08/07/millions-drop-off-food-stamps-under-trump-n2507310

108 https://www.WhiteHouse.gov/briefings-statements/trump-economy-booming-coast-coast/

People would be amazed and ask, *"how did they recover so easily?"* There are people in America pushing a strong socialist agenda, including key figures in the Democratic Party. During his February 2019 State of the Union Address, Trump said that the foundation of America was liberty and independence, and that America would never be a socialist country. Did Trump just make a prophetic statement? He also spoke about the 'miracle' of the U.S. economy with five million people coming off food stamps, unemployment at its lowest rate in half a century, and the creation of new jobs in manufacturing that most had said could never happen.[109] Is this another part of the prophecy on the way to fulfillment? On the 19th of January 2013, Clement shared what occurred that morning in prayer, and how God had revealed to him that the spiritual forces over America had planned the downfall of the American economy. The enemy was planning that non-profit companies and charitable organisations would close their doors and that people would lose their money. This prophetic word is confirmed by the Bible, which says that our battle is not against flesh and blood, but spiritual powers and wickedness in high places, and that the thief, Satan, has come to steal, kill and destroy.

On the 7th of August 2013, Clement prophesied that, in the soil of the United States, above and below, there was enough wealth to clear America's debt. On the 21st of June 2014, he prophesied the death to debt in the nation and on the 11th of April 2015, he prophesied a season of wealth coming to America. *"Death to debt is my promise but I need somebody else on the top."* This prophetic word was declaring not only prosperity for America but, God was going to influence or change things at the top, meaning the office of President. In another prophecy from the 15th of July 2015, Clement prophesied there were resources in the soil of America that

---

109 https://www.wnd.com/2019/02/full-text-trumps-2019-state-of-the-union-address/

could clear its debt.[110] CNN news reported on the 17th of November 2016, about a *"Mammoth Texas oil discovery, biggest ever in USA."* [111] On the 3rd of September 2005, Clement also prophesied about a new source of energy, that America would not have to rely on the Middle East for oil, and that they would be self-sufficient again. And on October 28th, 2006 he prophesied that there would be enough oil to make America independent. [112] Trump said during his 2019 State of the Union address that America was now the largest producer of oil and natural gas in the world, and the nation had now become a net energy exporter for the first time in 65 years. Could all this be related to these prophecies?

In June 2016, perhaps the first unthinkable event for that year occurred, and it was in Great Britain. The people of Britain voted to leave the European Union in what became known as Brexit. The prognosis of the experts was that Brexit would wreck Britain's economy, and it would destroy the positive work that had been done in previous years.[113] A *"vote for Brexit puts the existence of the UK in peril"*.[114] Just after the Brexit vote, two similar prophetic words were posted on the Elijah List website. On the 4th of July 2016, American Theresa Phillips wrote a word about an alliance between America and the United Kingdom, and the two nations would be allies in *"trade, tourism and industry."* The word said that the alliance would be strong, and the value of the American Dollar and the British Pound would increase. Coupled with this would be a revisiting of the past reformation and mass

---

110 Prophecies given by Kim Clement, 18th February 2011, 7th August 2013, 21st June 2014 and 15th July 2015. These are located at https://www.houseofdestiny.org/prophecy/

111 https://edition.cnn.com/2016/11/17/us/midland-texas-mammoth-oil-discovery/

112 https://www.elijahlist.com/words/display_word.html?ID=3406 and 28th October 2006 prophecy https://www.houseofdestiny.org/prophecy

113 https://www.businessinsider.com.au/brexit-will-destroy-everything-positive-about-the-british-economy-2016-7?r=UK&IR=T

114 https://www.euractiv.com/section/uk-europe/opinion/brexit-could-destroy-the-uk-as-we-know-it/

evangelism.[115]

Prophet Amanda Wells, posted a prophetic word on the 7th of July 2016. She wrote about a reformation coming, of a glory that would be greater than before, and Britain would be great again. The word then states that Great Britain's cities will *"shine with commerce and trade."*[116] Here we have two words regarding economic prosperity for England and one for the United States. Not only will both nations prosper economically, they will also experience a nationwide reformation, perhaps like the First and Second Great Awakenings of previous centuries.

Clement's prophetic word from the 15th of September 2006, contained something very specific possibly related to Brexit, although this wasn't known at the time. The word said there would be a sign related to the stepping down of the Prime Minister of Great Britain. The resignation of the Prime Minister would be a sign that something was going to advance out of Great Britain, and the United States. There would be a *"very unusual revival"*, and there would be an unusual breakthrough.[117] Britain's Prime Minister, David Cameron, who had campaigned against Brexit, resigned after the vote was in. Clement said that after the Prime Minister had stepped down, something would advance in both Great Britain and the United States. This ties in with the other prophetic words regarding the economy of both nations. Clement said there would be an unusual revival, which also ties in with the prophecies from July 2016. Here we have three prophecies, ten years apart, that all seem to line up with each other.

On the 27th of September 2018, the UK newspaper the Daily Express, reported President Trump and Prime Minister May from Britain had held talks for a free trade deal between

---

115 Theresa Phillips: America I have a birthday present for you, says the Lord. https://www.elijahlist.com/words/display_word.html?ID=16304

116 https://wellsministries.com.au/site/amanda-wells-britain-reformation-is-coming-with-a-far-greater-glory/

117 Kim Clement, 15th September 2006, https://www.houseofdestiny.org/prophecy

the two countries. The Prime Minister wowed business leaders in New York with plans for a Britain free of European Union *'shackles.''* [118] Could Brexit and the Brexit prophecies be connected to the February 2007 prophecy about the economy changing rapidly?

Point # 4: This point relates to the walls of protection around the country. The border wall with Mexico and restricting immigration from a small number of countries has become controversial. The fact that Trump has focused on border protection indicates that this could be connected to this part of the prophecy. And, if that is the case, then the opposition against these plans may be of a spiritual nature. There may even be a tactic to ignite people's emotions to give the message that one side of politics hates children, or hates people who are looking for a better life. Lance Wallnau calls this a manipulation of public sentiment, because there are companies in America who want cheap labour, and there are political groups looking for extra votes to keep them in power. This would indicate that the 'no borders / let the refugees in' argument, is more about money and power than it is about caring for the people.

Consider the picture that went around the world in June 2018 to highlight the separating of children from parents at the Mexican border. It was a photo of a crying two-year-old girl. Time magazine used the photo of this little girl, and one of President Trump standing over her, for its June 2018 cover. But it was fake news. The young girl in the picture was at the border with her mother.[119] Former Obama officials posted photos of children in detention centres on social media claiming this is what is happening now, yet the photos were of

---

118 https://www.express.co.uk/news/world/1023322/brexit-news-donald-trump-brexit-trade-deal-us-theresa-may

119 https://townhall.com/tipsheet/laurettabrown/2018/06/22/time-magazine-issues-massive-correction-to-story-on-family-separations-at-border-stands-by-cover-art-n2493509

children in detention in 2014 when Obama was President.[120] Despite the negative news coverage, a poll taken around the same time showed a (small) majority supported the President's decision to build a wall on the Mexican border.[121] The illegal immigration issue can be very controversial (and I hope I don't offend.) I'm sure there are genuine views on both sides of the debate, just as there are extreme views on both sides. However, there are some other points to consider in this.

Between October 2017 and February 2018, there was a 315% increase of adults falsely claiming children as their own to gain entry to the United States. Children have been separated from adults when the family relationship cannot be confirmed, where the child is deemed to be at risk from human trafficking, child abuse, or where criminal prosecution of the adult(s) is involved.[122] Separating children from parents (or adults) was a directive made several years ago, before Trump became President, to stop children from being placed in prison with adults, and to protect children from being exploited.[123] The recently appointed chief of border security said, that in her twenty-six years on the job, parents and children have always been separated when the law was violated.[124] A small number of children have deliberately been left behind at the border by their deported parents, who wanted their children to grow up in America. The separation of parents and children in this

---

120   https://www.businessinsider.com.au/migrant-children-in-cages-2014-photos-explained-2018-5?r=US&IR=T
121   https://www.thegatewaypundit.com/2018/06/poll-stunner-majority-with-trump-want-wall-built-migrant-families-deported-or-detained/
122   https://www.dhs.gov/news/2018/06/18/myth-vs-fact-dhs-zero-tolerance-policy
123   https://townhall.com/columnists/kevinmccullough/2018/06/17/why-the-left-always-lies-about-children-n2491563   and https://townhall.com/tipsheet/mattvespa/2018/06/21/amnesia-liberal-media-seems-to-forget-obama-separated-families-and-detained-ille-n2493020
124   https://www.bizpacreview.com/2018/08/12/border-patrols-first-female-chief-throws-mom-shaped-wrench-in-separation-narrative-im-a-parent-myself-663204

instance was instigated by the parents.[125]

Documents released by various government agencies in 2018 revealed that, some of the minors coming into the country were admitted murderers, rapists, drug smugglers, human traffickers and prostitutes. Minors have also reported about the abuse they have suffered.[126] The number of people who came into the country illegally, and who then committed crimes, numbers in the tens of thousands.[127] This includes forty-eight thousand charged with assault, five thousand for robberies, eighteen hundred for murder and five thousand for sexual assaults. And that's just for 2017.[128] The criminal gang MS-13 is also involved in illegal immigration, recruiting people at the Mexican side of the border, committing major crimes in the United States, while previously deported criminals constantly attempt to re-enter the country.[129]

There is another aspect to the uproar over children being separated from their parents at the border. In June 2018, President Trump had met with North Korea's Supreme Leader, Kim Jong-Un, in what was an historic occasion. This boded well for Trump. Two days after that meeting, the Inspector Generals office released a report, revealing there was political bias and collusion in the Department of Justice, and the FBI, to

---

125 https://townhall.com/tipsheet/cortneyobrien/2018/07/13/heres-why-the-hhs-couldnt-reunite-a-dozen-children-at-the-border-n2499822

126 https://townhall.com/tipsheet/katiepavlich/2018/07/11/documents-show-a-number-of-unaccompanied-minors-admitting-to-murder-for-cartels-other-crimes-n2498958 and https://www.judicialwatch.org/document-archive/hhs-records-unaccompanied-alien-children-fy-2014/?utm_source=deployer&utm_medium=email&utm_campaign=Press+Release&utm_content=20180711163937

127 https://townhall.com/tipsheet/mattvespa/2018/06/18/oh-my-thousands-of-illegal-aliens-arrested-for-violent-crimes-were-granted-daca-n2491688

128 https://townhall.com/notebook/stevesheldon/2018/07/28/leftists-hate-the-e-in-ice-n2500288

129 https://townhall.com/tipsheet/katiepavlich/2018/07/11/border-patrol-catches-another-ms13-members-claiming-asylum-n2499412

interfere in Trump's election campaign. They wanted to stop him from being elected, or to oust him once elected. Text messages exchanged by two FBI agents, revealed there was talk of trying to stop Trump from being elected and, if he was elected, they had an *'insurance policy.'* One of these agents had previously been appointed as part of the investigative team to investigate the alleged Russia Trump collusion. [130] A dozen staff from the FBI and the Department of Justice had been fired, resigned, demoted or retired. This was the bombshell from the Inspector General's report in June 2018 but, the story that dominated the news media, was the separation of children from parents at the U.S. border. It was like a deflection away from a real collusion story.

In October 2018, a migrant caravan numbering in the thousands, had moved into Mexico from Guatemala and Honduras. The aim of the caravan was to walk all the way through Mexico to the United States. There have been claims and counter claims as to how the caravan was organised. Vice President Mike Pence said he was advised by the President of Honduras, that the caravan was organised by left wing groups and political organisations in his own country. It was claimed that it was driven by human traffickers and left leaning political groups, using vulnerable people, and it contained criminal elements.[131] Mexican authorities reported that a second wave of the caravan included people armed with

---

130 https://townhall.com/tipsheet/mattvespa/2018/02/04/wsj-fbi-became-the-political-tool-of-anti-trump-political-actors-n2443905 and https://townhall.com/tipsheet/guybenson/2018/06/14/senior-fbi-agents-text-well-stop-donald-trump-from-becoming-President-n2490745 and

https://www.washingtonpost.com/world/national-security/trump-receiving-briefing-ahead-of-public-release-of-report-expected-to-criticize-fbi/2018/06/14/c08c6a5a-6fdf-11e8-bf86-a2351b5ece99_story.html?noredirect=on&utm_term=.bdbb54bf921c and

https://townhall.com/tipsheet/katiepavlich/2018/06/14/ig-clinton-investigation-n2465096

131 https://www.White House.gov/briefings-statements/interview-vice-President-pence-anna-palmer-jake-sherman-politico-playbook-live/

molotov cocktails, firearms, incendiary devices and rocks. They claimed the violent actions of this second group were those of criminals. President Trump meanwhile ordered the deployment of military troops to prevent access to America.[132]

Border Patrol agents used tear gas against the 'refugees' in November 2018. According to our own ABC, critics said the use of tear gas was overkill. [133] Yet this wasn't the first-time tear gas had been used. In 2013 under President Obama, tear gas was used against one hundred people who had thrown rocks at Border Patrol agents, when trying to cross the border from Mexico. [134]In Guatemala, authorities rescued seven children who had been taken by human smugglers working inside the migrant caravan.[135] Whilst the media and the Democratic Party have attacked Trump's stand on illegal immigration, conducting a Google search for Hillary Clinton, or Barack Obama, on protecting borders, will reveal videos of them declaring as recently as 2016, that America needed to protect its borders. In his State of the Union speech, Trump said tolerance for illegal immigration was not compassionate but cruel. The wealthy in America pushing for open borders, he said, live safely behind walls and gates. The influx of arrivals had added strains to schools and hospitals, reduced jobs and wages and seen increases in crime. One in three women coming across the border were sexually assaulted before they got to America. Children are used as pawns by human traffickers to exploit American laws, while young girls and women are sold into prostitution. [136]

---

132 https://www.wnd.com/2018/10/mexico-warns-of-molotov-cocktails-guns-in-2nd-caravan/

133 https://www.abc.net.au/news/2018-11-27/donald-trump-defends-use-of-tear-gas-mexican-border/10559208

134 https://www.sandiegouniontribune.com/sdut-border-patrol-rock-throwing-san-ysidro-2013nov25-story.html

135 https://www.judicialwatch.org/blog/2018/10/guatemalan-authorities-rescue-group-of-minors-from-human-smugglers-in-caravan/

136 http://www.wnd.com/2019/02/full-text-trumps-2019-state-of-the-union-address/

In February 2019, Trump signed a national emergency declaration, to fund building a border wall. He had asked Congress for $5.7 billion for the wall but the Democrat controlled Congress only granted him just under $1.4 billion. Since Trumps signing of an emergency declaration, total funding for the wall could now amount to $8.1 billion. The Democrats have claimed building the wall is immoral, racist, cruel or not needed because there is no national emergency. There is also the likely prospect that Trump's plans will end up being challenged in court. CNBC News claimed at the time of the national emergency declaration, illegal border crossings were at their lowest levels in a decade, and referred to 2017 statistics to support that position. Three weeks later, Fox News reported that for the month of February 2019, there were 76,000 people who had crossed the border, the highest monthly total in a decade, with up to one million people expected to arrive within the first six months of 2019.[137] With conflicting media reports, and claims and counter claims from wall supporters and wall opposers, it can be tough to try and figure out what is really going on. Clement's 2007 prophecy about a President building a wall of protection around the nation, gives us a spiritual and prophetic perspective to the issue. From that position, it does seem that the battle over the wall being built is not a battle between flesh and blood, but a battle against dark spiritual forces who only want to steal, kill and destroy.

On the 1st of October 2014, Morning Star Ministries founder, Rick Joyner, shared a prophetic dream that he had experienced. In the dream he saw a 'gate of Hell' that had

---

137   https://www.foxnews.com/opinion/tucker-carlson-1-million-illegal-aliens-at-the-border-is-a-crisis-manufactured-or-not   and https://www.cnbc.com/2019/02/15/as-trump-moves-to-declare-national-emergency-to-build-wall-border-crossings-at-record-lows.html   and https://www.cnbc.com/2019/02/15/trump-national-emergency-declaration-border-wall-spending-bill.html   and https://townhall.com/columnists/kevinmccullough/2019/02/17/the-five-definitive-reasons-trump-has-already-won-on-the-border-wall-n2541620

been opened (in the spiritual realm). These are 'gates' the armies of Hell use to enter a nation. The dream revealed to him that America's southern border was one such gate. Through this gate would come violent gangs and terrorists, which is now being reported. This didn't mean all the people coming through were evil, but that people with evil intent were coming through regardless. This prophetic dream adds another spiritual dimension to the border wall situation and the criminal element that is exploiting it. [138]

When we consider all these facts, it brings another perspective to the situation and another perspective to Clement's prophecy about a new President building the walls of protection around America. This is about protecting a nation from murderers, rapists, drug dealers and violent criminals. This is the role of governments according to Romans chapter thirteen. Rabbi Curt Landry writes that protecting the borders of a nation is *'for the righteous'* to keep evil out. Border protection is not anti-immigration or evil but, to protect a nation.[139] In our so called 'progressive' age, it's easy for people to take words out of context. So, I'm not saying that all the people trying to cross the border into America are criminals, but there are criminals amongst them. Secondly, there are legal ways to enter a nation, coming in through the 'back door' is not one of them. The battle is spiritual, and perhaps that's why we are seeing increased rage and rhetoric on this issue.

As already mentioned, Clement prophesied in July 2007 concerning a man of Irish descent being placed by God in the White House. We now know this to be Vice President Mike Pence. This prophecy also mentioned God's hand upon America and Great Britain, of God intervening in the media and burning out the dross, and how God will place in the

---

138 https://www.morningstarministries.org/resources/prophetic-bulletins/2014/prophetic-bulletin-border-war#.XDvRiPZuLIU

139 I'm going to reposition and realign this Government, Oct 4th, 2018, https://www.elijahlist.com/words/display_word.html?ID=20918

White House a man who will be transformed into a righteous believer. There will also be a time of peace and prosperity coming to America. Could this be the beginning of that time that was prophesied? We may be witnessing the beginning of prosperity in America, with the stock market hitting record highs and new jobs opening up, jobs that former President Obama said were gone. Could the conflict between Trump and several factions of the U.S. media, be God intervening in the media? Clement's April 4th 2007 prophecy states there will be an unusual change in the news media. Media organisations like Time Magazine and the TV show The View, will *"have no choice"* but to say what God wants them to say.[140] Perhaps this is also the beginning of something new for America and Great Britain. As ISIS is being defeated, could a time of peace be around the corner? The prophetic insight in Clement's April 2013 and February 2014 prophecies shed more light on recent events about the President with Hot Blood.

---

140 Kim Clement, April 4th 2007
https://www.houseofdestiny.org/prophecy

Chapter Five

The 2014 Prophecy

What we see and hear on the news can be very discouraging and fearful. Cindy Jacobs wrote in February 2017, that what we are seeing on the news is Satan discouraged and "very angry because of the things that he knows he's going to have to let go of." [141] As Kim Clement used to say, God is large and He is in charge. This means we have to decide whose voice we are going to listen to – the news media, or what the Lord is saying through the prophetic words given years in advance?

Clement prophesied in the 1990's that a 'burning bush' would lead America. He wasn't the only prophet to prophesy a Bush presidency but, he was one of two that I know of who prophesied that the election of Bush would come down to Florida. In the 2000 Presidential election, Florida handed George W. Bush the presidency, amid claims of Bush stealing the election. This was due to a disputed vote count that was resolved by the courts in January 2001. Clement prophesied in August 2000 (three months before the election, and five months before the court ruling) to watch what God was going to do in the political arena, that there would be a change the following year in the political realm, and the state of Florida was connected to this.[142]

Clement prophesied in October 2004, just before the

---

141 I am releasing reformation and awakening in the USA! What you see on the news is Satan very discouraged, Feb 17, 2017,
http://www.elijahlist.com/words/display_word.html?ID=17494

142 Prophecy by Kim Clement, 8 August 2000.
https://www.houseofdestiny.org/prophecy

November elections about a President breaking a record. [143] President Bush broke the records for his re-election, receiving fifty-nine million votes, the most for any President at that time. Around the same time, The Australian newspaper ran an opinion piece by a teacher of politics at the Australian Defence Force Academy, Malcolm Mackerras. He predicted that John Kerry, the Democratic candidate, would win the 2004 election against Bush by a landslide. He also predicted in October 2016, that Hilary Clinton had a 99% chance of winning the 2016 Presidential election.[144] At the end of the day, what the Holy Spirit is saying is more important than what the political experts, or the news media, are saying.

Clement's February 2014 prophecy about the next President, was just the next prophetic word in a series of words he had been giving, going back to 2007. On the 25th of March 2011, he gave a prophetic word regarding a President who was to come. It spoke of a future President who would have no fear and who would be decisive in making decisions. That sounds like attributes of Donald Trump. The prophecy contains what Clement would call clues to look for. It spoke of the *'restoration of America'* that would occur rapidly. Are the recent economic achievements part of this? It mentioned a new source of energy, medical breakthroughs and agreements with nations like China, and that people would say *"we never dreamed this would happen."*

The prophecy also says that in the middle of this presidency, healing would come to the nation, and that a woman who was once hated, but with beautiful eyes, would be instrumental in this healing. It will be a woman anointed of God and drug cartels will be afraid of her.[145] One clue is the

---

143 Prophecy by Kim Clement 24 October 2004
https://www.houseofdestiny.org/prophecy
144 http://www.switzer.com.au/the-experts/malcolm-mackerras---political-expert/99-chance-clinton-will-be-president/

145 Prophecy by Kim Clement, 25 March 2011,

middle of the presidency. If Clement's 2007 prophecy about a two-term President with hot blood is a major clue, and I believe it is, then the time period would be the middle of Trump's presidency. This could be around 2020-21. Who could this woman be? Former Vice President candidate Sarah Palin? The recent U.S. ambassador to the United Nations Nikki Haley? The First Lady, Melania Trump? Or perhaps another person?

Another clue is that the healing will occur because of deep hurt and divisions in the land. There cannot be a healing unless there has first been an injury. At the time of writing, many in the media talk about America being more divided as a nation now than at any other time in American history, except maybe the Civil War. John Fisher, a veteran in the Christian music industry, wrote in a column for Contemporary Christian Music magazine, that never in his life had he seen America so divided. He said it's Republicans against Democrats, gays against straights, citizens against immigrants, the haves against the have nots, males against females and blacks against whites. He said there is no middle ground anymore, there is no debate, no compromise, just vitriolic hatred, and whoever shouts the loudest, wins.[146] Kind of sums up society today not only in America but home here in Australia. Except that Fisher wrote this in 1995. It's only become worse since. I can recall people saying, George W Bush was responsible for the division in America, then it was Barak Obama who was responsible, and now its Donald Trump. Regardless of who, what or why, God has provided us with a future picture of hope, with the prophet saying that healing would come to the nation during the next presidency. That may seem a way-out prediction for those who see Trump's rhetoric as responsible for stirring up tensions but, maybe this has to happen in order for God to change the landscape.

---

www.houseofdestiny.org/prophecy
146 Holy Ground, John Fischer, CCM Magazine, March 1995, pg 78

On April 20th 2013, Clement gave an astounding prophecy. This is one of my favourites because, whilst prophecy can seem subjective, vague or full of symbolism, this particular prophecy was straight forward. It begins with naming two men, a Mr Clark and a man by the name of Donald. It then goes on to say that one of these men is proud of America and is an influential person who, because of his prayers, would become an influencer in America. God says *"as a king"* He will open the door this man has prayed about and he will be elected.[147] Isn't that interesting that the term 'king' was used in the prophecy. This usually applies to leadership such as governmental leadership however, as mentioned in chapter two, author Stephen Mansfield says Donald Trump was called 'king' by his father. I don't know who Mr Clark is, however, it is interesting to note that this prophecy was given three and a half years before Trump was elected. You can't make this stuff up. The beauty of modern technology means that prophecies like this one, were seen by thousands, and years later a vast crowd of witnesses can say we heard this back then. Consider how the person was described in the prophecy. He is someone who is a patriot (which is the term used in the ACPE prophecy for 2016), someone who is an influencer, someone who will run for political office, and whose first name is Donald. As a famous TV commercial once said, "But wait, there's more!"

Kim Clement's February 22nd 2014 "Prophetic Alert" prophecy, contains many nuggets or clues that point to this time period. There are a number of predictions in this lengthy prophecy, and you can find this prophecy at https://www.houseofdestiny.org/prophecy/. I will focus on a few key points from this prophecy: -

* A man singled out for the presidency.

* A man and a woman who would pray in the Oval office.

---

147 Kim Clement prophecy, April 20th, 2013
https://www.houseofdestiny.org/prophecy

* Gold and restoring the fortunes of America.
* Wall Street as a sign.
* California's drought.
* Calls to impeach the President.
* The revealing of top-secret documents.
* The new President will emerge in three weeks.
* Giving away Jerusalem.
* Changes to the Supreme court.
* God is going to deal with North Korea and the giant of debt

Point #1 A Man singled out for the Presidency: Here the prophecy is saying, a man had been singled out to be President of the United States, a man after God's heart. What does that mean, a man after God's own heart? Could that be Donald Trump? Recalling the story of the prophet Samuel going to anoint one of Jesse's sons to be the next king of Israel, the lesson Samuel learned that day, was that God doesn't look at what we see with our natural eyes. Even if one is doubtful that this could be a reference to Trump, I would ask that you indulge me as we continue through this prophecy.

Point #2 A man and a woman would pray in the Oval Office: I've already mentioned about President Trump praying with church leaders in the White House. Could Melania Trump's reading of the Lord's Prayer at a rally in February 2017, [148] be another clue about who this prophecy is related to?

Point # 3 Gold and a president who would restore America's fortunes: There are new drapes in the Oval Office at the White House and their colour is gold. Gold is also the colour of the Trump hotels. This could be another clue. When the rains came to California breaking the drought in January 2017, there was concern that the Oroville dam would break and flood the town of Oroville. Oroville gets its name from the Spanish word Oro, which means gold. The rains in northern California, and at the dam, washed away soil and revealed

---

148 http://www.foxnews.com/politics/2017/02/19/melania-trump-attacked-for-reciting-lords-prayer-at-campaign-rally.html

gold. This is an illustration of prophecy having more than one application. It also connects to a prophecy given in July 2013 by Johnny Enlow about gold being discovered in California. [149]

In relation to restoring the fortunes of the nation, consider these news reports from the start of 2017. Fiat Chrysler announced it would invest $1 billion into the U.S. economy, while Ford would invest $1.6 billion. Toyota would invest $10 billion over five years and Chinese retail giant Alibaba, said it would create over one million jobs, over five years. Walmart, IBM, Amazon and others said they would create tens of thousands of new jobs.[150] Add this to the economic highlights in the previous chapter, and I think we're starting to get some pretty big clues about who the prophecy is referring to.

Point # 4 A call to observe Wall Street and the number 20,000: This is telling us to watch Wall Street (the U.S. stock market), not to look to it, but to watch and observe, and also the number 20,000. This reference to 20,000, connects to another prophecy Clement gave on the 13th of March 2013, in which he referenced the number 20,000 seven times, how it would get to 20,000 *"sooner than most people think."* The prophecy also mentions people saying it would take many years to reach that number, but God was saying it would

---

149 https://www.sfgate.com/bayarea/article/gold-panning-oroville-dam-storms-erosion-10966360.php and https://www.elijahlist.com/words/display_word.html?ID=13165

150 http://www.foxnews.com/entertainment/2017/01/10/mike-rowe-revival-auto-manufacturing-goes-right-to-national-identity.html and https://www.breakingchristiannews.com/articles/display_art.html?ID=20188 and https://www.foxnews.com/politics/toyota-announces-10-billion-u-s-investment-days-after-trump-warning and https://www.breakingchristiannews.com/articles/display_art.html?ID=20189 and https://www.breakingchristiannews.com/articles/display_art.html?ID=20355

happen sooner than expected.[151]

The Dow Jones hit twenty thousand points on the 25th of January 2017, and then it reached 21,000 on the 1st March 2017, in what was described as the fastest one-thousand-point advance.[152] Since then, the Dow Jones has continued to make gains and has broken records over eighty times since Trump was elected. This surely has to be one of the strongest indicators that the 2013 and 2014 prophecies are talking about now. Prophecy equals tomorrows headlines today!

Point # 5 "California, a drought and God's sign of the rain: This part of the prophecy is talking about a drought being broken in California. It was a call to watch for the sign of rain, wind and severe weather, and that this would be a set up for God to pour out His Spirit. The drought in California was declared over on the 26th of January 2017. [153] There is something very interesting about this prophecy, because three things occurred within one week of each other that month. Trump was sworn in on the 20th of January, the Dow Jones reached 20,000 on the 25th of January, and California's drought was declared over for most of the state on the 26th of January. Three things mentioned in the prophecy all happening within the same week. It's one thing to observe events as they happen and ask is this a 'God thing?' It's totally another to prophesy them years in advance before they happen. But the prophecy does not stop there.

Point # 6 Calls to impeach the President and the revealing of top-secret documents when "another Snowden arises."

There are two points to look at from this part of the prophecy. Firstly, you have no doubt heard more than a few

---

151 Kim Clement prophecy 13 March 2013
https://www.houseofdestiny.org/prophecy
152 http://www.foxbusiness.com/markets/2017/03/01/dow-s-latest-1k-point-advance-ties-record-trump-policy-priorities-fuel-rally.html
153 https://www.cnbc.com/2017/01/26/the-worst-of-the-drought-is-over-for-california.html

media reports about people wanting to impeach President Trump. Clement prophesied in 2014 there would be people shouting for impeachment but the prophetic word was, it would not happen. The headline from USA Today in February 2017 said *'Time To Talk Trump Impeachment'*[154] and the headline from news.com.au on February 5th 2017 was *'Movement To Impeach Donald Trump Well Under Way.'* This was just weeks after Trump was sworn in as President. There is a webpage called *'impeachdonaldtrumpnow'* and there are Democratic members of the House and Senate calling for the President to be impeached.

In the lead up to the 2018 midterm elections, there was speculation and talk of impeaching Trump if the Democrats took control of the House in November.[155] After the Democrats took control of the House in the November election, the Democrats Chairman of the House Judiciary Committee, was overheard on the phone talking about plans to impeach Trump, and recently appointed Supreme Court justice Brett Kavanaugh. The Chairman was overheard by a reporter sitting a few rows away from him on a train.[156] An opinion piece in the New York Times two days after the midterm elections, called for Trump to be impeached.[157] One newly elected Democrat, after being sworn in, said it was time to *"impeach the mother f*******."*[158] And the media criticise Trump's rhetoric! Let's not forget the Russia Trump collusion investigation that was carried out, looking for a way to

---

154   http://www.usatoday.com/story/opinion/2017/02/26/Democratics-impeach-trump-gop-jason-sattler-column/98263054/
155   https://www.abc.net.au/news/2018-11-06/what-the-midterm-elections-will-mean-for-donald-trump/10462702
156   https://www.washingtonexaminer.com/opinion/oblivious-house-democrat-accidentally-reveals-plans-to-impeach-trump-kavanaugh
157   https://www.nytimes.com/2018/11/08/opinion/democrats-impeach-trump.html
158   https://www.theguardian.com/us-news/2019/jan/04/democrats-congress-trump-impeach-rashida-tlaib   and https://edition.cnn.com/2019/01/04/politics/rashida-tlaib-trump-impeachment-comments/index.html

impeach Trump. Yet, we have the prophetic word uttered years in advance, that impeachment will not happen! Take a look at the prophetic perspective given years in advance and then consider the cries of impeachment. The prophecy not only predicted that people would call for the President to be impeached, but also that God was saying this would not happen. The conclusion we could draw is that those demanding the President be impeached, whilst they may at best be sincere, are sincerely wrong. It may even say something about the accusers rather than the accused. Could it also be revealing corruption in the system?

As I wrote in Chapter Four, it's strangely interesting that in the same month the media 'broke' the story about the two-year-old girl allegedly taken from her mother at the border, a report was released from the Inspector General revealing that there had been political bias and collusion within the Department of Justice and the FBI. This was (a) to stop Donald Trump from being elected or, (b) to impede his presidency once elected. One of the FBI agents appointed to investigate the so called 'Russia Trump Collusion' conspiracy, was eventually fired when thousands of his text messages were released. These revealed he, and another agent, had been discussing *'an insurance policy'* in the event that Trump were elected, in addition to strongly worded politically biased text messages about Trump. [159]

Whilst government law enforcement employees are entitled to their own political opinions, they are nonetheless called upon in their respective roles to be neutral in carrying

---

159 https://townhall.com/tipsheet/mattvespa/2018/02/04/wsj-fbi-became-the-political-tool-of-anti-trump-political-actors-n2443905 and https://townhall.com/tipsheet/guybenson/2018/06/14/senior-fbi-agents-text-well-stop-donald-trump-from-becoming-President-n2490745 and

https://www.washingtonpost.com/world/national-security/trump-receiving-briefing-ahead-of-public-release-of-report-expected-to-criticize-fbi/2018/06/14/c08c6a5a-6fdf-11e8-bf86-a2351b5ece99_story.html?noredirect=on&utm_term=.bdbb54bf921c and

https://townhall.com/tipsheet/katiepavlich/2018/06/14/ig-clinton-investigation-n2465096

out justice. The same would apply, and should apply, to these agents if they had been talking about Hillary Clinton instead of Donald Trump. It's what we call the rule of law, everyone is to be treated the same under the law without partiality. We even find this in the Bible. In James chapter two, we are told that to show favouritism is to sin.

After two years, the so-called Russia Trump collusion investigation, failed to produce any evidence that the Trump campaign had worked with the Russians to stop Clinton from being elected. I originally wrote that I believed no evidence would be found in light of the prophetic word given years in advance, and because none exists. As I concluded my final tweaking of the manuscript, news broke from America about the Special Counsel's Report conducted by Robert Mueller. An initial briefing of that report was made public at the end of March 2019. Nineteen lawyers were employed in the investigation along with 40 FBI agents, intelligence analysts and other staff. As part of the investigation, 2,800 subpoenas were issued, 500 witnesses interviewed, 500 search warrants issued and 13 foreign governments were sent requests for evidence. That seems to be a very in-depth and meticulous investigation.

The conclusion was that no one from the Trump campaign 'colluded' with Russia to interfere in the 2016 election. However, the summary report did reveal what had been previously known; that Russian operatives had attempted to interfere in the election by sowing social discord, and that the Russians had hacked into computers or emails of people associated with the Clinton campaign, or organisations associated with the Democratic Party. The Special Counsel's Report did not recommend any further indictments however, in relation to claims of obstruction of justice by the President, Mueller stated that *"while this report does not conclude that the President committed a crime, it also does not exonerate him."* The Attorney General William Barr and the Deputy AG Rod Rosenstein, in relation to obstruction of justice, wrote that the Report did not identify any actions by the President that constituted obstruction, or that were done with corrupt intent.[160] Bottom line is the burden of proof for obstruction lies with the prosecutor and not the accused because of the presumption of innocence.

This doesn't mean that there won't be other attempts to impeach Trump. In fact, as the news broke about the Special Counsel's Report at the end of March 2019, there were still claims that perhaps Trump did collude with Russia, there were refusals to accept the findings of the summary report, someone said there was evidence that Trump was guilty, another asked how could Trump get off the hook, while a Congresswoman said, *"this is not the end of anything."* Top Democrats vowed to pursue further investigations into other areas of Trumps presidency.[161] The full report (except for the redacted portions that by law could not be revealed) was released on the 18th of April 2019. You can find the full 400 plus pages at https://www.justice.gov/storage/report.pdf. Again, no collusion and no obstruction of justice was the determination from the report. But that depends on which side of the media are reporting the story. For example, a conservative Townhall columnist said the good news was, there was no collusion to try and win the election with the assistance of a foreign power. Trump was understandably angry about the attempts to undermine him, but the legal issue over obstruction is now settled. The non-conservative Washington Post believed that the Mueller Report showed that there was evidence that the President had obstructed justice.[162] Other non-conservative, or

---

160 https://www.scribd.com/document/402974442/AG-March-24-2019-Letter-to-House-and-Senate-Judiciary-Committees-1#from_embed and https://www.heraldsun.com.au/blogs/andrew-bolt/massive-fake-news-fail-trump-cleared-of-collusion/news-story/543821a7af5d1ffb83bfc717bf61cec0

161 https://townhall.com/tipsheet/mattvespa/2019/03/24/trump-vindicated-mueller-report-confirms-no-collusion-and-the-liberal-media-is-n2543621 and https://www.usatoday.com/story/news/politics/2019/03/22/mueller-report-congress-oversight-investigations-trump/3061526002/

162 https://www.msn.com/en-au/news/world/mueller-report-lays-out-

Left leaning media outlets like CNN, were reporting that Attorney General Barr, who made the Mueller Report public, was the President's 'fixer' and that the final report was an 'inside job.'

The ancient Greek philosopher Aristotle observed that we will believe the views of someone we trust, despite the strong case to the contrary from somebody whom we dislike, or whom we suspect to be less than honourable.[163] This could explain why the mainstream media in the U.S. refused to accept the findings handed down after two and a half years of reporting constantly about the Russia Trump Collusion story. Jeremiah 17:9 says, *"The heart is deceitful above all things..."* This is why Jesus said we need to be careful who we listen to.

Will further investigations turn up anything new, or is this nothing more than a 'witch hunt' by people who can't accept the election result of 2016, as some media commentators claim? Time will tell. However, this prophecy about impeachment can be used in prayer as part of our spiritual warfare (1 Timothy 1:18), e.g. praying that impeachment will not occur and that the truth will be uncovered. We can add to that, the prophetic words given years in advance that point to Trump being President, the prayers of the saints calling out to God for their nation, and the mobilisation of Christians across the United States to vote in the 2016 election.

Legal and political analyst Gregg Jarrett, in his book *The Russia Hoax*, delves into the abuse of power at high levels in the FBI and the Department of Justice, to try to stop Trump from being elected. When that failed, they planned to sabotage his presidency by instigating an investigation, without facts or evidence, into his election campaign. Jarrett presents a case

---

obstruction-evidence-against-the-president/ar-BBW4Xtt?ocid=spartandhp and https://townhall.com/tipsheet/guybenson/2019/04/18/analysis-mueller-report-confirms-no-collusion-finds-aborted-obstruction-attempts-punts-on-charges-n2545026

163 Humilitas, John Dickson, Zondervan, 2011, pgs 41-42

that the FBI had already prepared a statement exonerating Secretary Clinton, before she was interviewed by them, over the use of an unsecured email server at her home. This was in breach of government regulations, was illegal, and occurred under Obama's presidency. Jarrett also investigated the millions of dollars in donations and speaking fees paid to the Clintons by Russians, and abuses of the law at high levels in the Department of Justice and the FBI. He also points out that there is no crime on the statutes in America called 'collusion.' He observed that it is not unusual for politicians, whether in government or opposition, to begin talking to foreign governments before an election.[164] His book is written from the perspective of someone who is a defender of the rule of law (i.e. no one is above the law), and he looks at the laws that were ignored or perverted. He claims that facts were ignored, and the media were baited with the claim that Trump had obstructed justice. If his book is on the money, then it would be a further indication that the battle we are seeing played out on our TV screens, is more than just 'resistance' or a 'witch hunt,' it is in fact a spiritual battle of epic proportions.

The second part of this section of the prophecy about impeachment says that another Snowden will arise. This is a reference to Edward Snowden, the former CIA employee, who released a large number of top-secret documents onto the internet in 2013. In March 2017, three years after the prophecy was given, Wikileaks released more top-secret CIA files onto the internet. One news headline said, *"Wikileaks Unveils Vault 7 – The Largest Ever Publication Of Confidential CIA Documents: Another Snowden Emerges."* [165] Prophecy gives us tomorrow's news headlines today, and here we have another clue as to the time period the prophecy is connected to. But there is more.

Point #7 *The new President will emerge slowly over*

---

164 The Russia Hoax, Gregg Jarrett, HarperCollins Publishers, 2018
165 http://www.zerohedge.com/news/2017-03-07/wikileaks-hold-press-conference-vault-7-release-8am-eastern

the coming three weeks. [166]

Twelve to fourteen days after this prophecy was given, being the 6th to 8th of March 2014, Trump spoke at the CPAC convention, a conservative political conference. Here he spoke about making America great again, which became his campaign slogan. Then on the 14th of March, which was twenty days after the prophecy (and within the three-week time period prophesied), Trump tweeted that whilst he wouldn't be running for Governor of New York State, he had *"much bigger plans in mind –stay tuned, will happen."* God does nothing without revealing his plans to his servants the prophets. Interestingly, in a prophecy given on the 11th of June 2014, Clement prophesied that there was going to be a change in the White House and *"America shall once again be great."* As Clement would point out, God gives us prophecy because prophecy is a higher perspective.

Point #8 Giving Jerusalem to Israel's enemies but God says no.

Here we have a comment about people wanting to give away half of Jerusalem to Israel's enemies, but God says this won't happen. Instead, God intends to do something in Jerusalem and the United States at the same time. I've previously mentioned the Cyrus Trump prophecy, the inaugural Cyrus/Trump coin, and Trump announcing the moving of the American embassy in Israel to Jerusalem. When announcing the embassy move, he mentioned that previous Presidents had promised to also do that but, had failed to follow through. He said he understood why when he began receiving calls from other world leaders advising him not to do it. Trump however, believed it was the right thing to do, and he followed through with his promise. Is this another clue from the prophecy pointing to the time period we are now in? Perhaps it is.

Then there is the matter of the Supreme Court, North

---

166 Kim Clement 22nd February 2014
https://www.houseofdestiny.org/prophecy/

Korea and the giant of debt, which were also mentioned in this 2014 prophecy.

Chapter Six

The Supreme Court Prophecy

Kim Clement's February 2014 prophecy mentions changes coming to the U.S. Supreme Court with two justices to step down from embarrassment. But God says he has plans to place righteousness in the highest court in the land, and even though there shall be attempts to put others in, God says he has the whole thing planned out. [167]

Conservative justice, Antonin Scalia, passed away in the first half of 2016 and was replaced in 2017 by a conservative, constitutionalist judge, Neil Gorsuch. A second judge announced his retirement in July 2018. This was 81-year-old Justice Anthony Kennedy; whose vote sometimes went either way. For example, he supported the legalising of same sex marriage in America in 2015. However, he also supported President Trump's travel ban in 2018. Depending on where you sit on the political fence, Kennedy either made good rulings or bad rulings. Neither of these two judges though had stepped down from embarrassment, so was Clement wrong? Not necessarily.

Remember the prophecy of Agabus that Paul would be handed over by the Jews to Rome. Paul did end up in Rome but, only after Roman soldiers rescued him from an angry mob intent on killing him. Remember too, the illustration that prophecy is like a lightning flash in a dark room. It's plausible that with the prophetic glimpse or vision he received regarding the Supreme Court, Clement saw two justices stepping down,

---

167 Prophetic Alert, Kim Clement, 22nd February 2014, https://www.houseofdestiny.org/prophecy

and interpreted it this way. That said, there may still yet be two justices who will have to step aside sometime in the future because of embarrassment that will arise. Time will tell.

It's what this part of the prophecy says, that is a possible key to the Supreme Court situation. God says he has a plan to place righteousness in the highest court and even though there shall be attempts to put other people into this court, God says he has it all planned out according to His will.[168]

At the announcement of Justice Kennedy's retirement, the Left and the media wailed that forty plus years of a woman's legal right to abortion, would be overturned because the President would appoint a prolife judge. They said this would give the Supreme the court the numbers to ban abortion. Brett Kavanaugh was the judge nominated by Trump in 2018 to replace Kennedy. A devoted Christian father who feeds the homeless, tutors under privileged children, and coaches youth basketball, he was labelled by some on the Left as a criminal and one who would pave the way to tyranny.[169]

As I began writing this book, a woman came forward claiming Kavanaugh had sexually assaulted her thirty-six years beforehand, when they were both teenagers. A letter about the assault, from the alleged victim, Dr Christine Blasey Ford, had been given to one of the Democrats on the Senate Judiciary Committee. This is the committee responsible for deciding which judges would be appointed to the Supreme Court. This letter, provided in July 2018, was kept under wraps until late in September when the committee was getting ready to vote on Kavanaugh's nomination. As one allegation was announced, other women came forward, and even a man, claiming Kavanaugh had committed sexually inappropriate acts against them, even though no one was able to produce

---

168 Prophetic Alert 22 Feb 2014, Kim Clement,
https://www.houseofdestiny.org/prophecy
169 https://townhall.com/columnists/timothyhead/2018/07/16/american-left-unhinged-by-a-christian-family-man-who-feeds-the-homeless-n2500837

conclusive evidence of any wrong doing. In fact, some of the witnesses whom the alleged victims named, denied knowledge of the events. A number of question marks began to appear in Dr Ford's testimony. She could not remember the date or the venue where the alleged event occurred, or how she got home. The alleged witnesses denied they were present, even though most of the media downplayed these discrepancies.

Meanwhile, protestors and those opposed to Kavanaugh's nomination, said women claiming they were victims of sexual assault, needed to be believed. That raises the question about Tom Robinson's trial in the novel To Kill A Mockingbird. Tom was a black man accused of raping a white woman, which the story reveals was a racially charged false accusation. This shows that the mantra 'women need to be believed' should not override the rule of law and the presumption of innocence. The sex crimes prosecutor, who questioned Dr Ford during her testimony, concluded that there was not enough evidence presented by Ford to take a case to court. [170] The interesting thing I noted following these developments, was that many on the conservative side of politics, and the media, even Kavanaugh himself, believed, something had happened to Dr Ford. They also believed there were too many inconsistencies in her testimony.

Kavanaugh himself denied the allegations against him, and two women, whom he dated before he was married, said, he acted like a gentleman on their dates. There were character

---

170 Ford's Ex Says She Lies, 4th October 2018, https://www.heraldsun.com.au/blogs/andrew-bolt/fords-ex-says-she-lies/news-story/d7739885ef69d683a8218ae88ec41e95

and Critics Of Brett Kavanaugh's Accuser Claim There Are 'Holes' In Christine Blasey Ford's story https://www.news.com.au/world/north-america/critics-of-brett-kavanaughs-accuser-claim-there-are-holes-in-christine-blasey-fords-story/news-story/2b18814be512fb08aab99f0c4cba4a3d and https://www.usatoday.com/story/news/politics/2018/11/05/brett-kavanaugh-allegations-report/1889770002/ and

https://townhall.com/tipsheet/leahbarkoukis/2018/10/09/cotton-schumer-political-operation-was-behind-this-from-the-very-beginning-n2526800

references for Kavanaugh from dozens of people, including over sixty women, which all showed a different person to the one being portrayed in the allegations. Kavanaugh produced a personal calendar from 1982 as evidence that he was nowhere near the place of the alleged assault. Feeling the heat from the Democrats questioning him, Kavanaugh, in very raised tones, addressed the committee and said they had turned the confirmation process into a national disgrace. *"You've replaced advice and consent with search and destroy."*[171]

Some claimed the sexual assault allegations was dirty politics, a delaying tactic to keep Trump's nominee from being appointed before the November 2018 midterm elections. Others claimed the allegations needed to be investigated, no matter how long it would take, and that women claiming to have been sexually assaulted must be believed. Whilst this was not a court hearing, to claim that the victim must be believed, and the accused not, goes right against the presumption of innocence, rules of evidence, the rule of law and centuries of legal precedent.

The activist watchdog organisation, Judicial Watch, filed a complaint to the Board of Professional Responsibility after the confirmation hearings were over. They claimed that Ford's lawyers had violated their professional responsibility. During the confirmation hearings, Dr Ford was asked if it had been communicated to her by her lawyers, or someone else, that the Committee was willing to come and interview her in private to hear her claims. When this question was asked, Ford's lawyers objected, claiming it was attorney-client privilege. Ford however, wanted to answer the question, and replied that had she known of the offer, she would have *"happily hosted you."* [172] In other words, her legal team may

---

[171] http://www.breakingchristiannews.com/articles/display_art.html?ID=25749

[172] https://www.judicialwatch.org/press-room/press-releases/judicial-watch-files-bar-complaint-against-christine-blasey-fords-lawyers/

have acted unethically by not relaying this offer to their client.

Media double standards were exposed when a man came forward around the same time claiming that Democrat Senator Cory Booker, had sexually assaulted him. During the Kavanaugh hearing, Booker made a speech about the responsibility of politicians to believe sexual assault allegations from survivors. Yet, when the story broke of Booker sexually assaulting a gay man, the media were strangely silent.[173] Now this may have been a smear and Booker may be innocent yet, this is the point. In Western nations we have a longstanding legal tradition of presumption of innocence, but quite the opposite was seen during the Kavanaugh hearing.

As the time for Kavanaugh's confirmation drew close, prayer warriors descended on Washington DC, where one journalist reported civility was low. The uncivil behavior was coming from members of the public opposed to Kavanaugh's confirmation. There were multiple instances of protestors taking over the offices of senators, and accosting lawmakers in hallways. These areas, that the media and the public generally had access to, were closed off around this time. [174] On the day the Senate voted to confirm Kavanaugh, protestors were ejected from the public gallery shouting, *"Shame, Shame!"* On the day that Kavanaugh was sworn in as the new justice to the Supreme Court, protestors turned up at the court pounding on the doors, wailing and gnashing their teeth, yelling, *"Shut it down!"* [175]

While the Senate confirmation process was underway,

---

173 Double Standard Seen As Media Stays Silent After Corey Bookers Accuser Comes Forward
https://www.faithfamilyamerica.com/double_standard_seen_as_media_stays_silent_after_corey_booker_s_accuser_comes_forward

174 http://www1.cbn.com/cbnnews/2018/october/if-we-show-up-god-will-do-the-rest-prayer-warriors-descend-on-capitol-hill-amid-kavanaugh-chaos

175 https://www.dailywire.com/news/36824/watch-leftists-protesters-freak-out-claw-supreme-emily-zanotti and https://www.heraldsun.com.au/blogs/andrew-bolt/kavanaughs-haters-are-deranged/news-story/6d00d11f3e86bd3503fcc4ae5d0e85da

Trump was attending campaign rallies only weeks out from the November midterm elections. People were attending in their thousands, with venues packed out. Dr Lance Wallnau noted that leftist billionaire George Soros was paying or funding groups to show up and protest, blow whistles and make a lot of noise. Trump, on the other hand, paid no one. Yet, wherever Trump went, the venues were packed out. Wallnau asked which of the two groups was reflective of a real grassroots movement?[176]

During the first week of October 2018, a few interesting things occurred in America. Brett Kavanaugh had already undergone six FBI investigations in the lead up to his Supreme Court nomination. Then the Democrats demanded a seventh FBI investigation after Dr Ford's testimony. The seventh investigation occurred during the first week of October. Some Democrats believed the FBI to be an impartial organisation, until the FBI delivered a conclusion that did not support their position.

At the same time this was occurring, Trump said he would continue to affirm equal rights and dignity for children with Down Syndrome. He said, *"All people are endowed by their Creator with dignity and the rights to life, liberty, and the pursuit of happiness,"* adding, *"I stand for life in all its beautiful manifestations."*[177] The U.S. Department of Health and Human Services new policy was released the same week, defining life as beginning at conception.[178] Trump also signed a bill with bipartisan support to provide greater protections for religious groups and their properties against government prosecution, and introduced penalties for damaging or destroying religious property.[179]

---

176   https://lancewallnau.com/what-you-did-not-hear/#more-20435

177 https://www.lifesitenews.com/news/President-trump-affirms-right-to-life-of-downy-syndrome-babies-in-new-state

178   https://www.christianheadlines.com/blog/u-s-department-health-human-services-policy-effect-declares-life-at-conception.html

179 http://www.breakingchristiannews.com/articles/display_art.ht

By the beginning of November 2018, Republican Senator Chuck Grassley, chairman of the Senate Judiciary Committee, had requested that four people who had made sex allegations against Kavanaugh, be investigated for making false claims. This included a woman and her lawyer, the man who accused Kavanaugh of assaulting him, and another woman, who had recanted her allegation of rape. She said that she was angry and had made the whole thing up to get attention and to hurt Kavanaugh's career.[180] A report by the Senate Judiciary Committee was released at the start of November. The four hundred plus pages of the report, included interviews with forty-five people and twenty-five written statements. It concluded that there was *"no evidence to substantiate any of the claims"* against Kavanaugh. Three of the people making allegations were referred to the Department of Justice and the FBI for investigation.[181] Kim Clement's 2014 prophecy about the Supreme Court adds a prophetic perspective to what unfolded on our TV screens. It reveals that the battle over a new appointment to the Supreme Court, was perhaps a spiritual battle.

Around the same time of Kavanaugh's nomination, abortion provider Planned Parenthood, were preparing an advertising campaign for New York, targeting Millennials to protect abortion funding. The ad, full of four-letter words ended with the phrase: - *"Protect our right to safely f— whoever the f— we want."*[182] The former President of Naral Pro Choice America, one cold January day in 2012, witnessed young pro-life marchers singing, praying and joyfully

---

ml?ID=25833

180 https://www.dailymail.co.uk/news/article-6348439/Kavanaugh-accuser-investigated-confessing-making-rape-claims.html and https://www.usatoday.com/story/news/politics/2018/11/02/brett-kavanaugh-accuser-referred-fbi-doj-investigation/1863210002/

181 https://www.usatoday.com/story/news/politics/2018/11/05/brett-kavanaugh-allegations-report/1889770002/

182 http://mobile.wnd.com/2018/07/defiant-planned-parenthood-f-anyone-who-fs-with-us/#6DF2Zutc9tBDOf1M.99

opposing abortion, marching through the snow. She realised then that the pro-choice movement was no longer recruiting the young. The Australian Christian Lobby believes we may be witnessing a similar situation in our nation. At a 2018 Meet the Candidates forum for a seat in the West Australian state parliament, five of the eight candidates expressed concern at the number of abortions in WA that are performed for convenience. Four of those five candidates were of the younger generation and ACL believes a generational change is gathering momentum.[183]

The Pro-life movement in America has grown from the grass roots since the 1970's using science, reason and medical alternatives, establishing pregnancy resource centres, and offering women alternatives to abortion. This has seen abortion centres close or abortion clinic staff resign. Some of the most prominent pro-life voices are women who have had abortions, former abortion clinic staff, and people who converted from pro-choice to pro-life.[184] We could add to this Christians praying for a miracle and prophecies that abortion will be overturned, remembering that prophecy should not be treated with contempt but instead we are to test it and hold onto what is good (1 Thessalonians 5:19-21). In addition, there was the undercover investigation in 2015 that revealed Planned Parenthood, the largest abortion provider in America, was not only selling baby body parts for profit (against U.S. law) but, also harvesting baby body parts, killing babies born alive from failed abortions to obtain them.[185]

---

[183] Australian Prayer Network newsletter, 4th July 2018

[184] https://townhall.com/columnists/shawncarney/2018/06/28/the-now-dire-threat-to-roe-v-wade-has-been-long-in-the-making-n2495503 and https://www.charismanews.com/culture/75794-the-unbelievable-story-behind-the-doctor-who-plays-an-abortionist-in-unplanned

[185] Planned Parenthood Horror Videos Investigation Underway As Congressional Hearing Begins 10 Sep 2015
https://www.breakingchristiannews.com/articles/display_art.html?

As I began writing this book, there were three anti-abortion movies in the making due to be released between the end of 2018 and 2019.[186] They have faced hurdles and challenges along the way, from having advertisements blocked, to record companies refusing to license songs for the movie soundtrack, to major newspapers refusing to review the movies and social media bans.[187] The first of these movies, Gosnell, is about America's worst serial killing abortion doctor, Kermit Gosnell. A grand jury report found he had killed hundreds of newborn babies born alive, by cutting their spinal cords. The movie about the 2011 arrest of Gosnell rated twelfth at the box office on its opening weekend in October 2018, and it made the top ten in its second week. Despite the movie doing well at the box office, approximately one third of cinemas pulled the movie.[188] Most major news outlets refused to review the movie, just as they had refused to send reporters to cover the court trial of Gosnell. I wonder if the cinemas will do the same for the Hollywood pro-abortion movies said to be in production? In March 2019, Unplanned, the true story of a former young abortion director who became part of the pro-life movement, was released. Despite a media blackout, the movie grossed more than double expectations, and came in at number five at the box office, for its opening weekend. Within

---

ID=16652 and Breaking: Planned Parenthood Caught In New Video 'We Make Fair Amount Selling Fresh Baby Eyes, Gonads, 15 Sep 2015,
http://www.breakingchristiannews.com/articles/display_art.html?ID=16678

186 https://stream.org/three-major-films-pro-life-themes-set-release-coming-months/

187 https://www.lifesitenews.com/news/facebook-blocks-ad-for-pro-life-movie-telling-the-true-story-about-roe-v-wa
and https://townhall.com/tipsheet/briannaheldt/2018/07/11/prolife-roe-v-wade-movie-facing-obstacles-including-cast-and-crew-walkoffs-n2497946/ and https://www.charismanews.com/opinion/in-the-line-of-fire/75340-hollywood-gives-abortion-an-r-rating and https://townhall.com/columnists/brentbozellandtimgraham/2019/04/05/trying-to-unplug-unplanned-n2544349

188 https://www.lifesitenews.com/news/theaters-dropping-abortion-expose-gosnell-blocking-ticket-sales-despite-bre

a few days, the movie had more Twitter followers than abortion provider Planned Parenthood, until Twitter suspended Unplanned's account, dropping its followers from 100K plus to just 151. Despite the focused opposition against Unplanned, over ninety abortion workers had left their jobs after seeing the movie, within the first few weeks of its release. [189]

What did we witness in the nomination process for Kavanaugh? An experienced judge, with ample qualifications for the job, being accused of sexual assault, and smeared by the Democratic party and much of the mainstream media. While all this was going on in September, there was a sound, and it was a call to prayer not only from Americans, but also from prophets in Australia. This was similar to 2015 and 2016 when various church leaders, prophets and intercessors, issued a call to prayer for the 2016 election. In a piece titled *"Overcoming Political Chaos, The Weapon Of Spiritual Warfare,"* Andy Sanders wrote that what was occurring in America at this time was an attack on anything that has Christian values attached to it, that gets too close to the political arena. He wrote that some of the events that had been occurring could end up being a big mistake for those who were behind it. [190]

Dutch Sheets, internationally recognised author, teacher and conference speaker, issued a call to prayer late in September 2018 for Judge Kavanaugh and the November mid-term elections. He believed America's destiny was at stake. Sheets was in the public gallery for Kavanaugh's hearing, and

---

189   https://www.breakingchristiannews.com/articles/display_art.html?ID=27448   and   https://www.bizpacreview.com/2019/04/01/unplanned-now-has-more-twitter-followers-than-planned-parenthood-739836   and http://www.christiannewswire.com/news/3575082444.html   and https://townhall.com/columnists/brentbozellandtimgraham/2019/04/05/trying-to-unplug-unplanned-n2544349   and   https://www.faithwire.com/2019/04/12/almost-100-abortion-clinic-workers-seek-to-leave-industry-after-seeing-pro-life-movie-unplanned/

190 Andy Sanders: "Overcoming Political Chaos! The Weapon Of Spiritual Warfare" Oct 3 2018
https://www.elijahlist.com/words/display_word.html?ID=20912#word-truncate

reported that America was under a demonic assault. *"The level of deceit, lies, slander, and arrogant pride was shocking, displayed not only by the protesters (sic), but also by opposing senators."* Sheets believed that what he witnessed was a spiritual war of *"historical proportions"* that will be felt worldwide. [191] CBN News reported in October 2018, that witches across America would be holding a spell casting ritual to put a hex on Brett Kavanaugh that month. More than ten thousand people had liked the 'Ritual to Hex Brett Kavanaugh' Facebook page. They also planned to continue casting spells to bind Donald Trump, following on from their efforts in 2017.[192] When Trump made comments about there being a witch hunt against him, he may have been speaking about the spiritual realm without realising it.

I come back to my main point that what we have been witnessing is a spiritual battle. Dutch Sheets also noted, as have many other Christian and media commentators, that the Democrats were using delay tactics during the Kavanaugh hearing, hoping that they would gain control of the Senate after the November 2018 mid-term elections. This would have enabled them to delay Kavanaugh's confirmation until the next Presidential election in 2020, when they hoped they would have a Democratic President at the helm. One of the prayer points raised was to pray that the truth would be exposed. Franklin Graham, evangelist and CEO of Samaritans Purse, warned that the 'God Haters' were out there after a cartoonist published a cartoon, showing Kavanaugh's ten-year-old daughter asking God to forgive her lying father. This was in response to Kavanaugh stating publicly that his ten-year-old daughter was praying for Dr Ford, the woman who had accused him of sexually assaulting her. American radio host

---

[191] America's Destiny Is At Stake: A Call To Pray For Judge Kavanaugh & Midterm Elections
https://www.elijahlist.com/words/display_word.html?ID=20870

[192] https://www1.cbn.com/cbnnews/us/2018/october/witches-launching-a-ritual-to-hex-brett-kavanaugh-still-working-to-bindtrump

Rush Limbaugh called the cartoon vile, disgusting, sick and despicable.[193]

To put it all together, the changes that have come to the Supreme Court appear to be what God had planned according to the prophetic word. Again, we come back to the axiom that God is large and He is in charge. Perhaps we are witnessing a convergence of events, coming from calls to prayer and prophetic words spoken years in advance. America now has a President who has been outspoken on the sanctity of human life. Changes have occurred in the Supreme Court, something prophesied in 2014 by Kim Clement in his prophecy about a new President. There are also prophecies, such as the 2016 ACPE prophecy, that point to a shift coming in relation to abortion laws. This convergence, this coming together, is not coincidence or even the end of the world and the beginning of tyranny. It's quite possibly the fulfilment of prophecy and a demonstration of who is God after all. (Hint – it's not governments, socialism, environmentalism, social justice causes, religion, people, things or events.) And if it is a God thing, then the opposition and uproar towards the new Supreme Court justices, is an indication of the spiritual warfare that has been going on over this appointment. The enemy has lost ground and does not want to yield it to God. He is fighting tooth and nail to hold onto it.

The U.S. Supreme Court appointments are very strategic and key for the United States. A majority of constitutionalist judges on the Supreme Court will ensure that the constitution is upheld, and freedom of speech and freedom of religion are protected for the next generation. The alternative is to yield the court to so called 'progressive' judges, who believe that the constitution is an evolving document, and can be interpreted according to current ideology, and not how it was intended by the founders. These 'progressive' judges would likely legislate from the bench

---

193   https://www.wnd.com/2018/10/franklin-graham-god-haters-now-fighting-kavanaugh/

instead of interpreting the meaning of the law. We may be witnessing something similar here in Australia. It seems that when laws are passed by so called 'progressive governments', or ruled on by so called 'progressive' judges, there has been a stripping away of rights and freedoms, for example, under the guise of discrimination or equality laws. Perhaps that season is coming to an end.

Chapter Seven

The North Korea Prophecies

Kim Clement gave many prophetic words regarding wars and terrorist attacks, although he wasn't the only one. The early 2000's saw a number of prophetic words given about the war in Iraq, including the Iraq war being over in 21 days (a Kim Clement prophecy) and the capture of Saddam Hussein. Clement prophesied Saddam's capture on 22nd November 2003, and a few days later on December 8th and 9th, Chuck Pierce and Dutch Sheets prayed for the spirit of witchcraft hiding the strongman, Saddam Hussein, to be broken. Another pastor present at that meeting prayed that the 4th Infantry Division would take the victory in capturing Saddam. Four days later on the 13th of December, members of the 4th Infantry Division captured him. There was a prophetic word given in 1998 by Dennis Cramer, in his book The Next 100 Years, about terror attacks coming to England. There was a warning for England to guard itself in the north east. The terrorist attacks that came in July 2005 originated in England's north eastern cities. Does God know a thing or two or what? Can a prophet know the plans of an enemy? Yes, they can. In 2 Kings chapter 6, God was revealing the plans of Israel's enemies to the prophet Elisha. God is still doing the same thing today.

In relation to North Korea, Clement and other prophets have prophesied regarding that nation, and how the two Koreas will become one nation. In Dennis Cramer's prophetic book, he writes that North and South Korea will unite quickly, and as the curse of communism is broken, crop production will soar.[194] In February 2003, Kim Clement prophesied that North Korea would plan to strike America, but God says it would be a mistake.[195] Fox News reported on July 5th 2006, that North Korea had fired five missiles: *"Long-Range Intercontinental Missile Fails."* One of the missiles aimed at the U.S. fell into the sea.

Shawn Bolz, author, TV host and minister, prophesied during 2004 and 2005, that there would be unification of the two Koreas. This unified nation would give to missions, stand with Israel, and will be used greatly before Jesus returns, in the areas of technology, engineering and science. Bolz believes that there is a seedbed of this greatness in North Korea. Already in one generation, South Korea has contributed to smart phone technology, reducing car emissions and water agriculture.[196] Chad Taylor prophesied in December 2004, that God would anoint a peacemaker between North and South Korea, and the barriers between the two countries would fall.[197] In July and October 2006, Kim Clement prophesied to watch North Korea as God would abolish the *"witchcraft and control"* in that nation. Between 2003 and 2015, Clement mentioned North Korea several times in prophecies he gave. For example, on the 27th of June 2009, he prophesied that God had already planned the downfall of Kim (likely a reference to Kim Jong-il, who died in 2011), and that there would be one Korea. On the 31st of December 2014, he prophesied not only would there be one Korea, but that God was going to bring *"the greatest revival"* to North Korea.[198]

Many years in advance, God was revealing through the

---

194 The Next 100 Years, Dennis Cramer, Arrow Publications, 1998, pgs, 92,93, 115 and https://www.elijahlist.com/words/display_word.html?ID=1828 and https://www.elijahlist.com/words/display_word.html?ID=1815

195 Kim Clement, 11th February 2003 www.houseofdestiny.org/prophecy

196 The Angel Over Korea & God's End Time Plan, 15th June 2018 https://www.elijahlist.com/words/display_word.html?ID=20327

197 https://www.elijahlist.com/words/display_word/2728

198 Kim Clement, 8th July 2006, 21st October 2006, 27th June 2009, 31st Dec 2014 www.houseofdestiny.org/prophecy

prophetic his plan for North Korea. Prophetic words like this give us not only insight, but hope. Around 2010 tensions were mounting on the Korean peninsula. I was a soldier in the Army Reserve at the time, and I remember at parade one night, one of the younger soldiers speaking about the situation in Korea. He was worried about a possible war erupting. I said there was nothing to worry about and it wouldn't be World War 3. That seemed to lift a burden off his shoulders. I jokingly added, Alan Alda, who played Hawkeye in the TV show MASH, had already signed up to do MASH 2 just in case. I had been listening to the prophets and I wasn't worried about a war breaking out. Whilst the enemy (Satan) might have been trying to influence situations to bring about a war, God had already spoken in advance and said that peace was going to come to that region.

Fast forward to June 2018, and something monumental took place when President Trump met with North Korea's Kim Jong-Un. It was an historic event. The Herald Sun front page headline called it the *"Deal Of The Century"*[199] According to the media narrative, Trump was going to start World War 3 because of the brash, non-diplomatic way he was handling North Korea, *"threatening fire & fury,"*[200] and referring to Kim Jong-Un as Rocket Man. (I don't know about you, but whenever I hear that phrase Rocket Man, Elton John starts singing in my head.) In a TV interview, President Trump said he felt foolish calling the North Korean leader names. He said he hated using the rhetoric but, previous governments had remained silent when North Korea made threats and boasted about what it was going to do. Trump said remaining silent wasn't the answer, and he had no choice but to use the tough rhetoric which then led to the peace talks. [201]

---

199 Herald Sun 13th June 2018
200 http://www1.cbn.com/cbnnews/politics/2018/june/President-trump-north-koreas-kim-wrap-up-historic-summit-kim-commits-to-complete-denuclearization
201 https://www.newsmax.com/politics/donald-trump-name-calling-and-rhetoric-north-korean-leader-kim-jong-un/2018/06/12/id/865574/

An interesting observation about this is, the peace talks took place seventy years after Korea became a divided nation in 1948. A biblical meaning for the number seventy is it relates to the number of nations. The year 2018 is also seventy years since the modern nation of Israel was formed. Seventy also relates to the fulfilment of Jeremiah's seventy years of captivity prophecy for Israel, and how a prophesied king by the name of Cyrus, was going to allow Israel to be re-established, and Jerusalem to be rebuilt. Now we have a modern-day Cyrus type king in the United States, who has an anointing to disarm kings. Could this be the time that North Korea and South Korea become one? The second meeting between Trump and Kim Jong-Un in February 2019 ended abruptly and seemed to be at a stalemate. However, one thing is certain, and that is, Trump has been the only American President to meet with North Korea, since the Korean War in the 1950's, to discuss peace. No one else has been able to do this. Could this be due to the Cyrus anointing that Lance Wallnau prophesied?

Kim Clement's prophecy from the 22nd of February 2014 says the future President that God has placed among them, would be the one who would deal with giants. In the prophecy Clement states people are asking how do they take down the giants of (national) debt, socialism and human secularism? The prophecy states that the people who reject this person (the President the prophecy is about) will be *"shocked at how he takes the giant down."* This is about giants in the land – socialism, secularism and national debt, being taken down. Ponder that for a moment. These three 'giants' are even crippling nations like Australia. Religious freedom is under siege from secularism and socialism. We have adults who have grown up with no knowledge of God or the Bible. And governments have raked up billions of dollars in debt. Could these giants be brought down?

The prophecy ends with God saying, He will go to the leader of North Korea and pay him a visit. Then God says to watch, and the sign will be the man he is sending will have a stone to take down the giant. [202] Is Trump the man with the prophetic stone for the giant(s) of socialism, secularism and debt, and perhaps North Korea? The first historic peace talks with North Korea occurred in the second year of Trump's presidency, and this last sentence in the prophecy, about the giant, says to watch for God's sign in relation to North Korea. We saw prophecy unfolding with the historic peace summit in June 2018, despite the pundits saying peace with North Korea could not be achieved, and the media saying Trump's actions would lead to World War 3. Was this a sign from God that a giant slayer was emerging?

Rabbi Curt Landry prophesied on September 28, 2018 that God was going to reposition and realign the government in America. He believed God was saying that something in the atmosphere had shifted and that Kim Jong-Un would even travel to America. When Kim Jong-Un comes to America, Landry prophesied that Kim will receive the Lord in the White House. God, he said, has raised up President Trump to raise up North Korea, and North Korea's resources will become part of the new economy that God is raising up.[203] That's an exciting prophecy and like all prophecy, will need to be judged. If it is good, hang onto it! Something else of interest is the spiritual roots in the family of both of these world leaders. Kim Jong Un's great grandparents were Christians and alive when Korea experienced a major revival in 1907. This revival led to Pyongyang, the current capital of North Korea, to be known as the Jerusalem of the East. Donald Trump's great aunts were the catalyst prayer warriors that brought revival to the Scottish

---

202 Kim Clement, 22nd February 2014,
www.houseofdestiny.org/prophecy

203 Curt Landry: "'I'm Going To Reposition And Realign This Government' Plus "Prophetic Words For The Nations" 4 Oct 2018, http://www.elijahlist.com/words/display_word.html?ID=20918#word-truncate

Hebrides islands in 1949-52. [204] Could it be that God has brought the 'sons of revival' together for something major?

And here's another clue that points to this time period, the Trump presidency and the peace talks with North Korea. In one of the last prophecies he gave, Kim Clement prophesied do not fear North Korea or Iran because *"in 2016 everything will change."* There would be the sounds of liberty and prayer coming from the White House with people asking God to intervene and, *"I shall, says the Lord."*[205] The man who wasn't supposed to be elected President in November 2016, who ran on a platform of life, *liberty* and faith, was elected. Since then, *liberty* has emerged in various forms as mentioned in chapter two, such as the establishment of the Conscience and Religious Freedom Division in the Office of Civil Rights, and economic liberty as mentioned in chapter four. And there are prayers occurring in the White House as reported by Christian and secular news agencies. This has not made things *'perfect'* or solved all of America's problems, but it does show that a change occurred in 2016 as the prophecy declared.

As Kim Clement once said, the future is not doom and gloom because, God has many great things planned. We shouldn't run away from the future, we should run to it! [206]

---

204 http://www.asianews.it/news-en/The-family-of-Dictator-Kim-Il-sung-were-devout-Christians-21409.html and https://www.worldtribune.com/desperate-prayers-by-trumps-aunts-in-sanctuary-cottage-said-to-spark-hebrides-revival-in-scotland/

205 Kim Clement prophecy, 29th August 2015, https://www.houseofdestiny.org/prophecy

206 Kim Clement, April 12th, 2014, The Den - Creative Miracles https://www.houseofdestiny.org/prophecy

Chapter Eight

The Demise of ISIS & Other Prophetic Words

Eruption, Lies in High Places and Exposure
On the 14th of June 2014, Kim Clement prophesied that America had entered a time of revealing and of the uncovering of lies in high places. This prophetic word says there will be a time when God will bring out from under the covers, the truth that had been covered up. In addition, there had been many lies in high places that had affected the world. He also prophesied that there would be an eruption *"under the earth"* in a national park in America. This would be a sign that God is going to contain the destruction that was trying to come upon America.[207] In July 2018, a volcanic fissure erupted at the famous Yellowstone national park.[208] Could this be the sign connected to the earlier part of the prophecy about lies being uncovered in high national places? Could it be related to the Russia Trump collusion investigation?

The Demise of ISIS

On the 17th of January 2015, Clement prophesied the sounds of victory and a global awakening, and a move of God's Spirit that would be unprecedented. Just stop and think

---

207 Kim Clement, Prophetic Alert, 14th June 2014, https://www.houseofdestiny.org/prophecy/

208 https://www.express.co.uk/news/world/1000808/Yellowstone-volcano-eruption-super-volcano-eruption-big-one-earthquake-USGS and https://nypost.com/2018/07/19/massive-fissure-opens-atop-yellowstone-supervolcano/

about that for a moment. A global awakening (to the message of Jesus) and a move of God's Spirit that is unprecedented.[209] Is that not a promise of hope for our future? It's not all doom and gloom. Yes, things are going to get worse before Jesus returns, the Bible is quite clear on that but, we in the 21st century are not the only ones to think that we are living in the days when Jesus could return. Revivalist preacher Jonathan Edwards reported in the early 1740's, that there were Christians in his day who thought that the time of the end was at hand. [210] Yet at this time, America experienced the First Great Awakening, an unprecedented move of God, and growth of the Christian faith, that impacted the soul of the nation. There was a Second Great Awakening in the early 1800's where again, Christians thought, based on the conditions in society at that time, Jesus was soon going to return. As a teenager and young adult, I read several books on the end times. The conclusion from the various authors was that the final countdown to the return of Jesus such as the rapture, was going to occur sometime before the year 2000. I scanned the pages of a book recently, published in 2012, that put forward its case for the final days to begin in 2016 but, here we still are. This may sound strange, and I'm not trying to date set, but I'm not getting ready for the rapture or the Second Coming any time too soon. I wonder if instead, we are going to witness a global awakening in our day, a subject that I have preached on a few times.

  In Clement's prophecy about a global awakening, there was also a word regarding the Islamic terrorist group ISIS, and how God was going to deal with them. In the prophecy he said ISIS had planned many things in Canada, and were present in the United States, Belgium, Germany, Turkey and *"all over Europe."* Remember, this was January 2015. Clement said as he was praying, he asked God to open his eyes, and he saw

---

209 Kim Clement, 17th January 2015
https://www.houseofdestiny.org/prophecy
210 Jonathan Edwards on Revival, The Banner of Truth Trust, 1995, pg 53

thousands of angels gathered to fight, just like Elisha saw in the book of Kings. He then asked the question *'do you really think that God is going to leave us alone?'* because the Earth belongs to the Lord! I have certainly questioned whether God has left us alone as miracles and answers to prayer seem to be a thing of the past. Despite the best efforts of organisations like the Australian Christian Lobby, who defend our religious liberties, (and who do a great job at it), we have lost ground in Australia, with laws passed, or considered in parliament, that have eroded our freedoms. I've observed Pentecostal churches become mainstream compared to what they were like thirty years ago. This is not a condemnation, just an observation. I could walk into an evangelical church service today and see little difference between it and a service at the Pentecostal church I currently attend. I watch the news and see the continuing rise of political correctness and activists pushing various agendas, and I think, "God, either you are getting ready to return, or you're getting ready to send an awakening." I like Clement's question in the prophecy, *"Do we really think that God would leave us alone"?* No, I don't think He would.

On November 13th 2015, there was a major terrorist attack in Paris, France when suicide bombers attacked a football stadium, and gunmen took hostages at a Death Metal concert. On March 22nd 2016, there were three coordinated terror attacks in Belgium at Brussels airport and a metro train station. Between March and June 2017, there were four Islamist terror attacks in England, including the Manchester Arena bombing that killed many children and teenagers. There were also three attacks involving vehicles being driven into pedestrians and the perpetrators stabbing people. Berlin, Germany suffered terrorist attacks in July and December 2016. A church was stormed in France in that year, and on July 16th, terrorists used a truck to kill people celebrating Bastille Day in France. Another attack occurred in Stockholm, Sweden on April 7th 2017. There was a shooting in Paris in the same month, and another vehicle used to mow down pedestrians in

Barcelona, Spain in August. In August 2018, an audio recording of an ISIS leader called for attacks in Canada. All the regions ISIS attacked were mentioned in the prophecy. God knows tomorrow, and the take away point from this prophecy is that not only is God going to deal with terrorism, there is also going to be a global awakening. That's hope!

In 2014, ISIS boasted tens of thousands of soldiers, with strongholds in Syria and Iraq but, three years later it was a shadow of its former self. During the 2016 election campaign, Trump promised to *"bomb the hell out of ISIS."* Under the previous Obama administration, the military was hamstrung *"with bureaucratic politically correct nonsense"*, but under the Trump administration, the military have a President who takes a hands-off approach. This enables the military to do its job - to defeat the bad guys. According to one general, the military are no longer second guessed, and they don't get twenty questions for every action they take, nor do they have to constantly call headquarters for permission. The result? At the end of 2017, ISIS' fighting force had been reduced from 35,000 to 1,000. The size of the territory it had controlled, had shrunk from 17,000 square miles to less than 2,000, while five million people had been liberated.[211] In February 2019, the war against ISIS was entering what one news headline called "the endgame" [212] as the last remnants held out in territory a fraction of the size they had conquered a few years earlier. The defeating of perhaps the world's most notorious terrorist organisation may bring protection not only to America but, like a stone dropped into water, ripple out around the world.

We can also add the 2015 prophetic word from Dr

---

211 https://townhall.com/tipsheet/timothymeads/2017/12/23/donald-trump-is-literally-wiping-isis-off-the-face-of-the-earth-n2426532 and https://www.latimes.com/opinion/op-ed/la-oe-abrahms-glaser-isis-assad-20171210-story.html#

212 https://www.theguardian.com/world/2019/feb/13/nothing-left-in-baghuz-isis-families-flee-as-war-enters-endgame

Lance Wallnau about Trump having the Cyrus anointing. The Cyrus anointing is to subdue nations and to strip kings of their power. It appears this includes an anointing to deal with terrorism. Here we have the convergence of prophetic words from different prophets that relate to the time we now live in. Only God could arrange that.

Cleaning up a mess

On the 14th of March 2015, Kim Clement was at Geneva, Switzerland broadcasting from there. Whilst he was talking, he said he felt like he was standing in 2017, in the time of a new American President and new administration, and he was sensing that people would be confused because what they had planned, didn't work. Their plans were going to be disrupted. What he could see however, was a strong figure in the United States saying he was going to clean up the mess. If there is one thing that stands out about Donald Trump, it's that he is a strong figure. We also know that his win in 2016 stunned not only America, but the world. On election night many media commentators thought Hillary Clinton had it in the bag, and that she was going to become the 45th President of the United States. Very few in the media thought she would lose, let alone the members of her own party, and the globalists that had supported her. Clement's prophetic word about things being disrupted, and people confused because their plans didn't work, not only shows that what occurred was a fulfilment of the prophecy but, it also shows that many people had overlooked the *"God Factor"* as Franklin Graham put it. During his first solo press conference in February 2017, Trump said he had *'inherited a mess'* at home and abroad. [213] The March 2015 prophecy was tomorrow's headlines today.

On September 7th 2013, Clement prophesied that it seemed another cold war between America and Russia was looking to come back. He said this meant another Ronald

---

213 Kim Clement, 14th March 2015, www.houseofdestiny.org/prophecy and I Inherited A Mess-Donald Trump http://thewest.com.au/politics/donald-trump/i-inherited-a-mess-donald-trump-ng-b88389533z

Reagan type figure would be raised up to deal with the nations of the world. This was going to occur at some point in time after Obama's presidency. [214] Is Donald Trump the Reagan type leader?

Blindfolds for Christians

One month before the November 2016 election, Australian prophet Lana Vawser released a word calling on the church to pray, because a horde of demons, (spirits of deception), had been released upon the earth, targeting the United States. Their task was to blind Christians in that country to the truth that God had anointed Donald Trump and Mike Pence to lead their nation. She said the election wasn't about Donald Trump and Mike Pence, his deputy. It was going to be about the destiny and future of the United States. [215]

During a podcast interview with Steve Strang of Charisma Magazine, Dr Lance Wallnau pondered if the Church in America was going to be awakened as to what they needed to do, to turn up to vote (for Trump). He said, *"Because, if history tells us anything (it's this), when God shows up, He's 'disguised' and His people don't (always) recognize Him."* [216] There have been many times in church history where this has been true. In the early nineteenth century for example, using organs in a church service was considered a radical idea and some resisted it. Charles Finney, a great American revivalist preacher of the mid nineteenth century, allowed women to pray in public meetings and would call people to the front for prayer, something now commonly referred to as the altar call. But, back in Finney's time, allowing women to pray publicly, and having altar calls, was considered a radical practice, and it drew criticism from previous revival leaders. The issue of 'speaking in tongues'

---

214 Kim Clement, 7th September 2013,
https://www.houseofdestiny.org/prophecy
215 Pray for Discernment: A vision of the spirit of deception over the US elections https://www.elijahlist.com/words/display_word.html?ID=16770
216 https://www.elijahlist.com/words/display_word.html?ID=16740

was still being debated for and against in mainstream churches when I began attending a Pentecostal church in 1982. Some considered speaking in tongues as a gift only for the early church, or worse, it was 'of the devil.' The point is, Lance Wallnau is correct, sometimes God shows up and we don't always recognise Him.

Justice Prophecies (a work in progress?)

I've called the following two prophecies a work in progress as at the time of writing, they appear to be about future events that have yet to unfold. Australian prophet Lana Vawser released two prophetic words during September 2018. In the first, she writes that *"the King of Glory is stepping in with a roar of justice."* She goes on to write about a *'great rearrange'* coming, many walls of opposition falling and a tidal wave of God's justice being displayed.[217] In the second word she wrote about an encounter with the Lion of Judah (another name for Jesus) standing over the United States, and He was roaring. This roar was to release the fear of God, and the world would know God's great love and power, which would open the door for a great harvest of souls (the coming Awakening). Then she heard the Lord say that all delays are broken, and delays attempting to hinder what God has planned would suddenly come to nothing.[218]

Whilst these words do not specifically mention the Supreme Court nomination or the midterm elections, or the Russia Trump collusion investigation, the timing of their release lines up with other words calling the church to pray at that time for a breakthrough in America. Another Australian prophet, Christy Johnston, posted a prophetic word with a call to intercede for the American midterm elections. In it she writes that the Lord said, *"Let my justice prevail."* God will be

---

217 https://lanavawser.com/2018/09/21/i-heard-the-lord-say-united-states-of-america-get-ready-for-another-major-demonstration-of-my-power/

218 Lana Vawser: "United States Of America - The Lion Of Judah Is Stepping In And Breaking Delays!" Sept 26, 2018,
https://www.elijahlist.com/words/display_word.html?ID=20878

cleaning up things, hidden things would be brought into the light and God's justice will prevail. Media moguls are going to fall, and she called for prayer that any hidden agendas would be exposed, and the lies and confusion of the media to be exposed and torn down.[219]

Bringing chaos to a violent level

Hank Kunneman is the senior pastor of Lord of Hosts Church, and founder of One Voice Ministries based in Omaha. During a church service on the 14th of October 2018, Hank, who has been recognised as one who ministers under a strong prophetic anointing, prophesied that in the coming days there were going to be protests, violence and bloodshed in America because there were people who ruled with wicked spirits. However, there was a flame beginning on the West Coast like it did in the days of the Jesus Movement of the early 1970s. Interestingly, Kim Clement prophesied more than once about a new type of Jesus Movement beginning in California. Kunneman encouraged people to not think that God has lost control due to the mobs that will arise because, a *"righteous rebellion"* is beginning to form. The prophecy then continues with a word about corruption, pedophilia and treason being uncovered, how classified documents will be released, and that emails that some claim do not exist, will be brought out. Accusations, arguments and hatred will be exposed and the truth of things will become evident. The final part of the prophecy speaks of people who have been paid and briefed on what to do should the Democrats lose the November mid-term elections, *'deceit to bring chaos to a violent level.'*[220]

This prophecy was given on the 14th of October, and perhaps one could claim that violence was already occurring in America. There were the violent protests after Trump was

---

219 Christy Johnston: "The Media Giants Are Falling! A Call To Militant Intercession and For The Midterms" Sept 17, 2018,
http://www.elijahlist.com/words/display_word.html?ID=20832

220 Prophetic Warning for America Given by Hank Kunneman 10 14 2018 www.youtube.com/watch?v=dHHeaTa8B7M

elected and sworn in as President. There was the shooting of Republican Steve Scalise and the other threats of violence and actions previously noted. Yet, when we take a spiritual perspective that our battle is not against flesh and blood but *"against the rulers, against the authorities, against the powers of this dark world and against the spiritual forces of evil in the heavenly realms"* that Ephesians 6:12 speaks of, then we can respond not from fear or rage but we respond with prayer, fasting, worship, loving our enemies, praying for their salvation, and for their deliverance from the evil schemes of the enemy. The people committing the acts of violence are not our enemies because this is a spiritual battle.

Then there is the approach predicted by Hollywood actor James Cromwell. Speaking at an awards ceremony on the 28th of October, Cromwell said that if the Democrats did not win the mid-term elections, he predicted there would be *"blood in the streets"* if they couldn't stop Trump.[221] On the 4th of November 2018, the Democrats Maxine Waters said during an interview, that protests are about making people feel uncomfortable. *"Speak what you heart is telling you to do."* [222] These statements came two to three weeks after Hank Kunneman's prophecy about violence being planned if the Democrats did not win the election. Here we have a prophetic word given in advance, warning about violence coming but, in that word, there is also hope. Firstly, being warned about impending violence is a call to pray for God's intervention, and for the enemy's plans to be thwarted and exposed. The second part of hope in the word is that a flame (meaning a revival flame or move of the Holy Spirit) will arise, a new Jesus Movement. The third part of hope is the exhortation to

---

221 Actor James Cromwell warns of revolution: There will be blood in the streets if Democrats lose.
https://www.washingtontimes.com/news/2018/oct/30/james-cromwell-actor-warns-of-revolution-there-wil/

222 https://ntknetwork.com/waters-on-violent-protests-protests-is-about-making-you-feel-uncomfortable/

not be worried about the mobs, or to think that God has lost control, because a *"righteous rebellion"* is arising. The tables are going to turn. And finally, there is going to be exposure of hidden agendas, corruption and things kept secret. Jesus speaks of the exposure of hidden things in Mark 4:22. Perhaps this could be the time for that to happen.

I keep coming back to the position that this is a mammoth spiritual battle unfolding in front of our eyes. In the words of Kim Clement, *"God is large and he is in charge!"* We don't have to be despondent in all of this. Previous generations had to face in the 1940's, Japanese military aggression in the Pacific, and Nazi dominance in Europe. For my generation, we grew up under the fear of global communist expansion, the threat of nuclear war and global catastrophe caused by pollution. Previous generations have felt it was the end of the world as well, and lived with the same type of fear and distrust that is prevalent today. But they got through it all, and evil in the end was defeated. There is hope, hope, hope for our God is an awesome God!

The Mark Taylor Prophecy

I don't know much about former firefighter Mark Taylor. However, he claims that God revealed to him in 2011, that God had chosen Donald Trump to bring restoration, respect and honour to America. He prophesied about the economy and America's relationship to Israel becoming stronger, things that have certainly improved since Trump was elected. [223]The Trump Prophecy movie was released to cinemas in the U.S. in October 2018, and will probably be available on DVD at some stage. Taylor has also written a book about his prophecies from 2011.

---

223 https://www.charismanews.com/politics/issues/61220-firefighter-prophet-updates-his-vision-for-donald-trump-s-presidency

Lance Wallnau Prophecy

Lance Wallnau lists eleven prophecies about Donald Trump, predicted in 2015 before he was elected, in his short e-book Cyrus Trump. Some of these I have already covered such as the Left will manifest, Trump being the wrecking ball to political correctness and the Cyrus anointing. Other topics covered include Trumps success will depend on the unity of the church and those appointed to advise him, an economic reset and a time of clashing. There is a link to this at the end of this book. His other book, God's Chaos Candidate, is also worth reading.

Chapter Nine

Hope for Tomorrow

I don't need to say that Donald Trump has offended people, or given cause for people to question if he is really cut out for the job of President, let alone be the one God may have chosen to lead the United States. American columnist, Michael Brown, writes that Trump is not the Saviour because he did not die for our sins, only Jesus did that. He then lists some of Trump's achievements, and concludes that the political alternatives to Trump, gave him little choice to vote for anyone but Trump, or his party. He confesses that he does not like the President's rhetoric at times, and that he thinks it may actually cause more division. But, he adds, the media have been divisive and destructive, and some of the Democratic party policies, such as identity politics, are also divisive, so there is blame on all sides.[224] As they say, when we point the finger, there are always four more pointing back at us.

This book isn't about Donald Trump's behavior or comments, real or perceived from the past, or his rhetoric in the present. Major news networks, on both sides of the political divide, pulled a TV commercial just days before the November 2018 midterm elections. They claimed it was racist as it inferred that all of the people in the migrant caravan heading towards the U.S. border, were criminals. This commercial had been authorised by Trump personally. Bombastic, racist and divisive are some of the words we have probably heard to describe Trump, yet those who work closely

---

224 https://townhall.com/columnists/michaelbrown/2018/11/05/midterm-talking-points-for-protrump-evangelicals-n2534862

with the President describe him as someone who is respectful, who listens, is empathetic, thoughtful and caring.[225] I have read the latter over and over again from those who get up close and personal to Trump. What does this tell us? It tells us that sometimes we can be judgmental, especially when we judge from a distance, or by the what the media are telling us. Sometimes we might be right in our conclusions, sometimes we might be wrong, and that is challenging. It challenges me with the words I say and use because, sometimes I have said or done things that have been inappropriate, or that I have regretted. Haven't we all? In an interview, Trump admitted that maybe his tone and rhetoric for the previous two years could have been softer. He said he would love to get along, however when you are criticised, you have to hit back.[226]

Here's something that we tend to overlook in the debate over Trump's rhetoric, and that is the rhetoric that is already coming from the opposite direction. When Trump announced he was going to run for President, the media mocked him and thought he wasn't serious. When protestors yell *"f*** Trump"* and celebrities want to punch him, or blow up the White House, and Democrat politicians endorse uncivil behavior, then there are plenty of examples of inappropriate speech. Yet, do we hear the media criticising the protestors, or the celebrities who have used four letter words, or made inappropriate comments about Trump? The double standards, and the hypocrisy, are blatant. As a society, we have moved away from the words of Jesus of Nazareth, who said to love our neighbor as our self, and to treat others the way we would want to be treated.

---

225 http://www1.cbn.com/cbnnews/politics/2018/july/lsquo-we-don-rsquo-t-trust-russia-nikki-haley-lowers-the-boom-on-putin-puts-iran-on-notice and https://www.newsmax.com/newsmax-tv/sean-spicer-the-briefing-press-secretary-inauguration-crowd/2018/07/23/id/873336/ and http://www.faithwire.com/2018/07/02/senator-shares-shocking-thing-trump-told-him-about-race-that-gave-him-hope/

226 https://www.newsmax.com/newsfront/tone-rhetoric-resistance-racial-card/2018/11/05/id/889469/

On the eve of the 2018 midterm elections, Trump stopped his speech at a packed-out arena because a woman near the front of the stage had fainted. He asked if there was a doctor in the house and told the first responders not to rush, and to take their time. He watched on and waited almost ten minutes until the lady was taken out of the arena before resuming his speech. At one stage, he asked the crowd to say a prayer, and then singing broke out with the crowd singing Amazing Grace.[227] I like the opening lyrics to this song because it is such a leveler when it comes to people. *"Amazing Grace, how sweet the sound, that saved a wretch like me. I once was lost, but now I'm found, was blind but now I see."*

There has been a lot to take on board in this short book. I believe it's worth considering these prophetic words, with some spoken well in advance of the events. Not only have the prophecies come to pass, they add the *"God Factor"* to the story that is unfolding right in front of our eyes. It gives us another perspective to what we see and hear on the news. We need to be careful who we listen to as Jesus said in Mark 4:24. It should mobilise us to pray *'thy will be done on earth as it is in heaven.'* Perhaps we could also mobilise to be more active about the threats to our own nation coming from political correctness, and Leftist activist driven agendas. Agendas that are seeking to limit free speech, freedom of religion, even parental rights, while at the same time, indoctrinating our children, our future, to embrace ideologies that twenty years ago, neither side of politics would have embraced.

I hope the prophecies mentioned in this book provide spiritual insight into what we see and hear on the six o'clock news. Perhaps they will confirm for us that not only is this a spiritual battle, but also that God has not gone to sleep. He is very much alive and active in current world events, as He has always been. For me, that's exciting. I hope too that you will

---

[227] https://dailycaller.com/2018/11/06/trump-rally-breaks-into-chilling-rendition-of-amazing-grace-as-trump-pauses-for-fainting-woman/

be able to pray for our political leaders, rulers and kings (including President Trump). Paul writes in 1 Timothy chapter 2, to pray for our leaders, because this is good and is pleasing to God. No matter what our political affiliations as Christians, we are called to pray for those in authority. Pray for God's hand to be upon them and their decision making. Ask God to bless them according to His plans and purposes for their life. Ask him to bless their relationships with their spouse, children and family. Pray for their health, for advisors who would have wisdom, for good plans to prosper and for our nation to prosper. Let's be slow to criticise. Pray for our current Prime Minister, whoever it may be when you are reading this book. I've heard many Christians say its good to have a Christian Prime Minister, like Scott Morrison, and it is. But just because someone is a Christian, it does not mean they automatically qualify as the best person for the job. Perhaps its better to have someone who is anointed by God for the task instead. That's not a judgment against certain politicians but perhaps it is a worthwhile principle.

After reading this book I would consider it mission accomplished if you could take away hope. As Kim Clement used to say, *"These are the end times, but they are not the end of time, so we need to occupy until He comes."* Looking forward to the return of Jesus is not something we should be ignorant of as Christians but, we need to be careful that we don't fall into *"end time-itis"* as Johnny Enlow calls it, which causes us to withdraw from trying to influence our world. Our Christian forebears across the globe in previous generations believed Jesus would return in their day but, they never gave up the fight. Because of their Christian worldview, they fought for freedom, for the abolition of slavery, for voting rights for women (in Australia, Margaret McLean, a Melbourne Baptist), and they established kindergartens, schools and universities to educate all people, and not just rich males. They influenced art and literature, they brought about changes to work place laws to protect women and children from being exploited, they gave us world changing inventions like Morse Code, the aeroplane and the discovery of genetics. They campaigned against injustices, like the poor treatment handed out to aboriginal people, or for civil rights in America. They limited the power of kings, and gave us our Westminster parliamentary system of government. These things happened because our Christian forebears moved beyond the four walls of the church. They became politicians, educators, scientists, and inventors. They reformed prisons, mental health care and caring for the poor and sick. Shouldn't we be trying to continue to influence and change society, to stand up to injustice, and defend the rights of free speech, freedom of association and freedom of religion? Are there giant slayers among us who can take down the giants of political correctness, or school indoctrinating programs like Safe Schools, or the attacks on religious liberty? Is this too hard for our God?

God changed the playing field in America with Donald Trump. Now it's our turn in the land down under. We proudly say in our churches (and sing), this is the great southland of the Holy Spirit but, it won't be as long as we remain disengaged from society. Jesus commanded us to go into the world, to share the good news and to disciple nations. We have to go into government, that's part of going into the world. We have to go into education, the arts, media, sports, in short, we have to go into culture. We can't afford to remain disengaged from what is happening in our nation any longer. We have to speak out and be ready for confrontation with world systems that seek to oppress us. In the 1700's, the American colonists rose up against the oppression of King George of England. Leading the voices and shaping public opinion were the clergy. Galatians 5:1 tells us that Christ gave us freedom and we should not allow ourselves to be made slaves again. We are going to have to stand up for our rights, like previous generations have done. We must not pull back for the soul of our nation is at stake.

The election of Donald Trump has reverberated around

the world, shaken things up, and divided opinion, even in the church. Yet, it has positively affected the American economy. It has brought about the appointment of many judges at all levels in the court system, who will interpret the law rather than legislate from the bench. Regulations have been passed in the U.S. to protect freedom of religion, freedom of speech and the rights of the unborn. God has played his prophetic Trump card, and even though we Aussies don't live in the USA, we may soon be beneficiaries because of what is occurring in the spiritual realm.

We can make a change in the government of our nation by way of our prayers, our votes, our letter writing, being involved in politics and so forth. Plenty of other groups do it, so why not us? Or have we forgotten the Proverb that says, when the righteous rule, the people rejoice? Our religious liberties in Australia have been under siege for many years, and at the time of writing they continue. But, we can change it because the saints who have gone before us believed they could in their day. A minister by the name of Josiah Quincy wrote in the Boston Gazette in 1767, as America faced oppression from England, that with God, they would not fear the hour of trial coming upon them, but would defend their civil and religious liberties, and even though they may be outnumbered, *"yet the sword of the Lord and Gideon shall prevail."* [228]

At the end of October 2018, Brazil elected Jair Bolsonaro as their new President. Most of the media labelled him a far-right candidate, in part because of alleged, or actual, disparaging remarks he made about women, gays and minorities. I'm not here to defend inappropriate comments, that would be silly, but it would seem that part of the reason for Bolsonaro's success was that he took a stand against a corrupt establishment. He stood up to Latin American socialism, promised to tackle corruption (what Trump would

---

228 The Light & The Glory, Peter Marshall and David Manuel, Revell Publishing, 2009, pg 322

call draining the swamp), to fix the economy, tackle the increasing crime rate, and move Brazil's embassy in Israel to Jerusalem. According to the Christian news network CBN News, it was evangelical Christians who helped get Bolsonaro elected.[229] Associated Press picked up on this, weeks before the election in a piece titled *'Evangelicals, Growing In Force, To Impact Elections.'*[230]

As I reflect on this, I'm wondering if there are there similarities between what happened in Brazil to what happened in the election of Donald Trump? One similarity is that people are rising up against the establishment, something that happens time and again throughout the pages of history. Is this all happening now because of the God factor? Lance Wallnau said that, when God shows up, the church does not always recognise him. When the Charismatic renewal hit the church in the late sixties and early seventies, there were some in the church who rejected it. When Christian singers began to embrace modern styles of music in the seventies, there were leaders in the church who criticised it as being too worldly and of the devil. I believe Wallnau is correct in his observation. We can miss it when God does something that is out of the box that confronts our theology, our doctrines, beliefs and opinions.

To put it another way, look at the things Donald Trump has achieved in his first two years in office. He has defended the Christian faith in various ways, from defending people's rights to say Merry Christmas, to appointing judges who will uphold the American constitution. Twenty key principles of religious liberty have been issued to the Department of Justice. Trump stands for the rights of the unborn and the disabled. Church, aren't these the things we stand for? Shouldn't we be voting for political parties or people who will stand for these?

Lance Wallnau wrote before Trump was elected that he

---

229 http://www1.cbn.com/cbnnews/cwn/2018/october/how-evangelical-christians-helped-elect-brazils-new-President

230 https://apnews.com/bef042d5f5c94bd484987b3494564a5d

would be the wrecking ball to political correctness. Perhaps one of the biggest battlefield arenas where we are seeing this played out, is in the confrontations with the media. Kim Clement prophesied that the economy would change under a new President. It's happening. He prophesied that Wall Street would break records. It's happening. He prophesied that the new President would build a wall of protection around the nation. It's beginning. He prophesied the new President would have people wanting to impeach him. It's happening. He prophesied that the new President would be the one through whom God would place righteousness into the highest court in the land. It's happening. Lance Wallnau prophesied that the Left would manifest and Trump would be blamed. It's happening. He also prophesied that Trump would carry the King Cyrus anointing - think the Trump/Cyrus coin minted in Israel. He said he would carry an anointing that would deal with terrorism and disarm other kings, think North Korea and the defeat ISIS has suffered. He said he would deal with the economy and religious freedom. It's happening. The ACPE prophesied that 2016 would be the year the tide would turn. It happened. They prophesied that God would raise up a patriot to be the next President. It happened. We are seeing new trade deals that benefit America, the pulling out of the Paris Climate Accord, and decisions that put America first to *"make it great again."*

    Jesus of Nazareth told us to judge a tree by the fruit it produces. Think about this fruit and consider whether or not it is a good thing? Since Trump was elected, over five million new jobs have been created, including 600,000 new manufacturing jobs. Almost five million people have come off food stamps, a form of welfare in America. Unemployment is at its lowest levels in half a century for all demographic groups including African Americans, Hispanics, women and people with disabilities. More red tape has been cut in two years than any other administration was able to do during its total time in office. America is now a net exporter of energy. Trump is concerned about the drugs and criminals coming across the southern border along with the sexual assaults against women, and children used as pawns to exploit American laws by human traffickers. ISIS have suffered devastating defeats and at the time of writing, they were less than a shadow of their former self. We may not like the messenger or how he delivers it, yet the fruit of his works and the values he stands for are hard to ignore.

As I consider all of these things and the prophetic words that have been made regarding an American President, and how the evidence points to Donald Trump, I believe we have seen the God factor at play. Amos 3:7 says God does nothing without revealing his plans to his prophets. Does it make sense? Maybe not, it depends on our worldview or our theology. Not everything makes sense to those of us who only 'know in part' as the Apostle Paul writes. Yet, something is happening around the globe and it is building momentum. Perhaps it is the God factor after all. And if it is the God factor, then there is hope!

Recommended Reading

God's Chaos Candidate, Dr Lance Wallnau, Killer Sheep Media Inc, 2016

Cyrus Trump – 11 Prophecies About Donald Trump Predicted In 2015, Dr Lance Wallnau, www.lancewallnau.com

The Russia Hoax, Gregg Jarrett, Harper Collins, 2018

Donald Drains The Swamp, Eric Metaxas and Tim Raglin, Regnery Publishing, 2018

Choosing Donald Trump, Stephen Mansfield, Baker Publishing, 2017

The Seven Mountain Prophecy, Johnny Enlow, Creation House, 2008

Secrets of the Prophetic, Kim Clement, Destiny Image Publishers, 2005

Call Me Crazy but I'm hearing God, Kim Clement, Destiny Image Publishers, 2007

Kim Clement prophecies can be found at www.houseofdestiny.org/prophecy

About the Author

Randell Green has had a diverse career working in the finance and health insurance sectors, Christian radio, the church, and he has served in the military as a Reservist. His ten-episode segment series, Impact, stories of Australia's Christian past, was made available to 150 community radio stations by the Community Radio Network in 2015.

He has also been a community volunteer for over thirty years, volunteering in church youth work, Police Blue Light Discos, a roller rink DJ, multi-award-winning community radio programmer, Christian music magazine contributor and many other community activities.

Randell lives in Traralgon, Victoria and is married with three children and one grandchild.

e: greenrbooks@gmail.com

p: P.O. Box 996 Traralgon, Victoria, 3844

www.ingramcontent.com/pod-product-compliance
Lightning Source LLC
Chambersburg PA
CBHW072054290426
44110CB00014B/1675